PROVING SAFETY

WICKED PROBLEMS, LEGAL RISK MANAGEMENT, AND THE TYRANNY OF METRICS

GREGORY SMITH

PROVING SAFETY

GREGORY SMITH

WAYLAND LEGAL PTY LTD
AUSTRALIA
2024

For more information contact:
gws@waylandlegal.com.au
www.waylandlegal.com.au

ISBN - Paperback: 123456789
First Edition: April 2024

About the Author

Greg is an international award-winning author and qualified lawyer who has spent more than three decades specialising in safety and health management. Greg works with clients helping them to understand their responsibility for safety and health and develop processes to discharge those responsibilities.

In addition to being a lawyer, Greg has worked as the Principal Safety Advisor for a major oil and gas company and General Manager Health and Safety in a transport and mining services company. Greg holds various board positions and taught the Accident Prevention unit at Curtin University in Western Australia.

Greg is the author of, *Management Obligations for Safety and Health* and *Paper Safe: The triumph of bureaucracy and safety management*, co-author of, *Risky Conversations: The Law, Social Psychology and Risk* and the editor of *Contractor Safety Management*, which won the 2014 World Safety Organisation's Educational Award.

Contents

PART 1
BACKGROUND

Reliance placed by Esso on its OIMS for the safe operation of the plant was misplaced. The accident on 25 September 1998 demonstrated in itself, that important components of Esso's system of management were either defective or not implemented. If the implementation of OIMS by Esso was to be measured by the adequacy of its operating procedures, they were deficient and failed to conform with the ECI Upstream Guidelines or with the OIMS System Manual. If it was to be measured by reference to the actions and decisions of those persons who were attempting to resolve the process upsets on 25 September 1998, they were also deficient. The deficiencies were in the manner in which Esso dealt with the acquisition and retention of knowledge. This involved its training system, its operating procedures, its documentation and data system, and its communication systems.[1]

---

[1] Esso Australia Resources Ltd ran several gas plants in south-eastern Victoria, Australia to process gas from wells in Bass Strait. On Friday, 25 September 1998, a vessel in Gas Plant 1 fractured, releasing hydrocarbon vapours and liquid. Explosions and a fire followed. Two Esso employees were killed, and eight others were injured. Supplies of natural gas to customers in Victoria were cut off. In response to the disaster, the Victorian government established a Royal Commission to report on the causes of the explosion and fire. Dawson, S. M., & Brooks, B. J. (1999). The Esso Longford Gas Plant Accident: Report of the Longford Royal Commission. Melbourne: Parliament of Victoria at [13.42] (**Longford Royal Commission**)

Background

In 2018, I wrote a book called *Paper Safe: The triumph of bureaucracy in safety management.*[2] The book came about because of my ongoing frustration in being involved with clients who:

- had a serious workplace accident;
- had apparently sophisticated and comprehensive safety management systems in place; however
- those systems were substantially disconnected from any intended safety purpose.

Very often, my frustrations were compounded when the organisation's own safety management systems, designed to manage workplace health and safety hazards and risks, were used against the organisation as evidence of their failure to meet their legal obligations.

I will regularly be referring to workplace health and safety management systems throughout this book, and in this context, I need to point out that, at least for the purposes of the book, I am "*systems agnostic*". I do not care how an organisation "*does*" safety just so long as the organisation can demonstrate that their workplace health and safety management systems "*work*".

From a legal risk management perspective, if your "*system*" does not rely on documented processes and procedures but rather you grant workers the discretion to "*vary locally*", the court will not really care. Similarly, if you manage safety by requiring strict adherence to safe working procedures, the court will not really care about that either. From a legal risk management perspective, the only real question is: *did your system to manage work health and safety risks "work"?*

Do you have "*proper*" systems to manage the hazards arising from the business and do you have "*adequate*" assurance to know if the proper systems were implemented and effective to manage hazards?[3]

Organisations were (and still are) investing heavily in work health and safety documentation without any real understanding about whether:

- documentation would be beneficial to manage workplace health and safety;
- the documented processes were implemented; or
- the documented processes were, in fact, effective to manage workplace health and safety risks.

---

[2] Smith. G. (2018) Paper Safe: The triumph of bureaucracy in safety management (**Paper Safe**).

[3] I have discussed the content of a "*proper*" system and "*adequate*" assurance in detail in Part 4 the Legal Framework.

A key theme of Paper Safe was to highlight the extent to which it seemed that safety management systems had devolved into bureaucratic, tick and flick exercises in administration, quite disconnected from, if not the hazards in the workplace, at least the workers. To borrow from the Longford Royal Commission:

> *Evidence was given that [Operations Integrity Management System (OIMS)], was a world-class system and complied with world best practice. Whilst this may be true of the expectations and guidelines upon which the system was based, the same cannot be said of the operation of the system in practice. Even the best management system is defective if it is not effectively implemented. The system must be capable of being understood by those expected to implement it.*
>
> *Esso's OIMS, together with all the supporting manuals, comprised a complex management system. It was repetitive, circular, and contained unnecessary cross referencing. Much of its language was impenetrable. These characteristics make the system difficult to comprehend both by management and by operations personnel.*
>
> *The Commission gained the distinct impression that there was a tendency for the administration of OIMS to take on a life of its own, divorced from operations in the field. Indeed, it seemed that in some respects, concentration upon the development and maintenance of the system diverted attention from what was actually happening in the practical functioning of the plants at Longford.*
>
> ...
>
> *Reliance placed by Esso on its OIMS for the safe operation of the plant was misplaced.*[4]

Paper Safe was not a criticism of paperwork per se. Certainly, it was not a manifesto calling for the abolition of all paperwork as an adjunct to helpful workplace health and safety management. With the benefit of hindsight and reflection – although not expressly stated in the book – Paper Safe was protesting the lack of critical thinking in workplace health and safety management; the failure to examine our workplace health and safety initiatives rigorously and critically to meaningfully assure that they were fit for purpose, implemented as intended, and effective to manage workplace health and safety.

---

[4]   Longford Royal Commission at [13.38] – [13.42].

It also seems that this question of purpose, implementation, and efficacy still arises in the "*New View*" of safety. Indeed, there does not appear to be anything inherent or intrinsic in any of the collection of New View ideas that makes it any more suitable for demonstrating effective workplace health and safety management systems or for demonstrating effective legal risk management.[5] In saying this, I am not saying that New View safety might not be a better way to "*do*" safety – I think the jury is still out on that question – I am just saying it offers no better framework for evidencing that it "*works*" than anything that has gone before it.

An area that Paper Safe did not explore in detail was the "*metrics*" used by organisations to track workplace health and safety and to "*measure*" if their workplaces were "*safe*".

This idea is what I intend to explore in this book.

My basic proposition is that workplace health and safety is an archetypal "*wicked problem*" which does not lend itself to measurement or metrics. The metrics we do have, along with (what appears to be at the time of writing) the ongoing development of "*new*" metrics, all appear to have (or are likely to be afflicted by) the same problems that afflict safety management more generally. Namely, the slide into bureaucratic exercises of administration, devoid of assurance and critical thinking.

My argument is that at their core, organisations, and especially their leaders, are passive recipients of safety information, most notably safety metrics. Organisations and their leadership do not critically challenge safety information.

Lag safety indicators – "*lost time*" and other injury rate data has long been identified and criticised as being a wholly ineffective measure of the "*safety*" of an organisation. This is a proposition with which I agree, but my position on lag indicators has softened over the years, which is an issue that I will explore and explain later in the book.

In response to the well-known (and frequently cited) weaknesses of lag indicators, the health and safety industry has embarked on the pursuit of so-called "*lead indicators*". However, the evidence to date, at least when it comes to practical implementation, suggests very strongly to me that lead indicators take the issue of proving safety no further.

I first encountered the idea of lead indicators in around 2007, when after practising law for about 17 years, I went to work in an oil and gas

---

[5] When I refer to the "*New View*" of safety in this book I am referring generally to the broad range of ideas and philosophies that have emerged from the related concepts of high reliability organisations, resilience engineering, safety II, safety differently and most recently human and organisational performance.

company. At that time, the significant and thought shaping BP Texas City Refinery explosion, which occurred on 23 March 2005, was garnering the attention of the health and safety industry worldwide.[6] The final investigation report by the US Chemical Safety and Hazard Investigation Board[7] found, amongst many other things, that:

> *Reliance on low personal injury rate at Texas City as a safety indicator failed to provide a true picture of process safety performance and the health of the safety culture.*[8]

The Chemical Safety Board Inquiry also picked up on recommendations of a parallel report, the Baker Panel Report[9] noting:

> *The report's 10 recommendations to BP addressed providing effective process safety leadership, developing process safety knowledge and expertise, strengthening management accountability, developing leading and lagging process safety performance indicators, and monitoring by the Board of Directors the implementation of the Baker Panel's recommendations.*[10]

While lag indicators still have a predominant (and wholly unjustifiable) position in most larger organisations' workplace health and safety reporting, lead indicators are also very common.

Some commentary, especially when describing *"new"* indicators of safety performance, would appear to have people believe that lag indicators are the only measure of workplace health and safety, and hence, their new approach.

This is not true.

Lead indicators are common and have been around for decades. They just do not seem to add any value in practice.

Examples of lead indicators that I have seen over the years include:

- percentage of safety conversations completed against target;
- percentage of toolbox attendance completed against target;

---

6   On 23 March 2005, the BP Texas City refinery experienced a catastrophic accident. At the time, it was one of the most serious workplace disasters in the United States for nearly two decades, resulting in 15 deaths and more than 170 injuries (**BP Texas City**).

7   U.S. Chemical Safety and Hazard Investigation Board. (2007). Investigation Report. Refinery Explosion and Fire BP Texas City. Texas City: U.S. Chemical Safety and Hazard Investigation Board (**Chemical Safety Board Inquiry**).

8   Chemical Safety Board Inquiry, p. 25

9   Baker, J. A., Leveson, N., Bowman, F. L., Priest, S., Erwin, G., Rosenthal, I., ... Wilson, L. D. (2007). The Report of the BP U.S. Refineries Independent Safety Review Panel. Retrieved December 24, 2017, from http://www.csb.gov/assets/1/19/Baker_panel_report1.pdf (**Baker Panel Review**)

10   Chemical Safety Board Inquiry, p. 28.

- percentage of high severity event investigations completed;
- achieving a safety climate survey score of greater than 3 out of 5 during a project;
- completion of audits against audit schedule;
- percentage of critical control verifications completed against target;
- percentage of procedures reviewed on time against target;
- percentage of corrective actions closed out on time;
- number of high potential injury incidents;
- number of significant injury events;
- percentage of leader safety observations completed against target; and
- percentage of training completed against target.

The problems with lead indicators in my view fall broadly into three categories.

First, most lead indicators are based on multiple, critical assumptions which are never overtly described or tested.

Second, nearly all workplace health and safety lead indicators are based solely, or predominantly, on:

- measuring activities – how many times do we do the thing, or what percentage of things have been completed; or
- bureaucratic compliance – has the form been filled out correctly?

Most, if not all lead workplace health and safety metrics in my experience, do not have any qualitative evaluation in relation to the *quality* of the activity performed or its *effect* on workplace health and safety.

Third, lead indicators are never measured or assessed for efficacy. Does the activity achieve the outcome it was designed to achieve and contribute to, or improve, the health and safety of the workplace?

Of course, once you introduce a metric into an organisation it immediately becomes susceptible to *"corruption"*, so that the pursuit of the successful metric quickly becomes more important than the safety intention the metric was designed to measure. The *"process"* (i.e., achievement of the metric) becomes more important than the *"purpose"* (i.e., the safety initiative). Indeed, in many cases it appears that the process becomes the purpose, so that the only reason workers and supervisors participate in the safety initiative is to contribute to the metric. The safety outcome is secondary – if it is relevant at all.

When I talk about organisational or institutional corruption, I am talking about the pressure an organisation can bring to bear to achieve an outcome it desires. I am not using the term *"corruption"* in this context in a pejorative sense, nor do I suggest that it is a deliberate or targeted strategy – although it can be.

By way of example at the simplest of levels, if an organisation requires workers to complete three safety observations a shift (such as a Take 5), then it can exert pressure to ensure that this outcome is achieved. However, by exerting pressure to ensure that a specific outcome is achieved – three safety observations completed a shift – it can create trade-offs or compromises which undermine the specific outcome. In the case of safety observations, the pressure to ensure that a certain number of safety observations are completed each shift often leads to a *"corrupting"* process whereby workers will complete the safety observation before they arrive at the worksite, or complete them in bulk, or treat them as a mere *"tick and flick"* exercises without having any regard to the actual workplace health and safety issues that the safety observation is designed to address.

This disconnect between purpose and process is a key concept I explored in Paper Safe, specifically in the context of safety related paperwork. It is in the completion, collection, and collation of safety related paperwork that we see workers and supervisors mechanistically completing the safety paperwork not for the possible safety benefits it is supposed to provide, but because it is a *process* that they will be held accountable against.

In the case of metrics, this distinction between purpose and process has a particularly insidious effect insofar as it contributes to an illusion of safety.

When I talk about an illusion of safety, based on my experiences with organisations, I am talking about the illusion that arises when organisations and their leaders uncritically assume that workplace health and safety indicators in health and safety reports are measures of the state of *"safety"* in their organisation, when in reality, they are not.

Lead workplace health and safety indicators, at best, are seldom more than a measurement of activity done in the name of workplace health and safety. Their efficacy in achieving safety outcomes is a question both unasked and unanswered.

These are all concepts I will explore further in the book.

For the sake of clarity, and before we proceed too much further, I should get on the record and say that I am, and remain, wholly unconvinced that any lead safety indicators provide very much, if any, insight into the state of workplace health and safety management much less the more difficult to define idea of workplace safety. There may, I accept, be some lead indicators that have the potential to provide insights into narrow, technical aspects of safety. There are, moreover, experts far more qualified than I who can talk about the underlying conditions necessary for health and safety in the workplace, and I remain open to the objective evidence for, and the quantification and measurement of, these underlying conditions. But, as I say, I am, currently, unconvinced.

One area, however, where I do feel I can speak with a level of confidence and authority, is the objective demonstration of safety in the context of legal proceedings, and in this context, both lead and lag indicators are all but irrelevant.

I have long ceased to be surprised by the aspirational and moral pronouncements of the health and safety industry that legal compliance is an organisation's "*minimum*" standard. But surely, if legal compliance was an organisation's minimum standard, then the pages of workplace health and safety data in the monthly health and safety reports could easily be held up in defence of a prosecution under workplace health and safety legislation?[11]

No?

If all our workplace health and safety indicators in the monthly health and safety report are green, surely that is compelling evidence that our organisation has done everything reasonably practicable to ensure the health and safety of workers and others?

No?

If our workplace health and safety reporting and metrics cannot meet even our *minimum* legal requirements, how, with any level of critical thought, can we believe this information tells us anything about the state of safety in our workplace?

---

[11] When I am referring to workplace health and safety legislation in this book, I am generally referring to Australian work health and safety legislation as described in the current Model Work Health and Safety Act (https://www.safeworkaustralia.gov.au/doc/model-work-health-and-safety-act) (**Model WHS Act**). In 2008 Australia commenced a process to try and "*harmonise*" workplace health and safety legislation across the country. Before 2008, each Australian State and Territory had its own health and safety legislation, administered by its own health and safety regulator, and overseen by its own system of courts or tribunals. The process culminated in the Model WHS Act which has been adopted over time, and in different degrees, by all jurisdictions in Australia, except Victoria. Unless it is necessary to refer to a specific piece of health and safety legislation for technical detail, in this book I will be referring generally to either "*work health and safety legislation*" or the Model WHS Act.

The short answer, I think, is that it cannot and that our approaches to understanding and evidencing safety in the workplace are fundamentally flawed.

So, where to from here?

The purpose of this book is to provide a framework by which organisations and its leaders can build an arguable position to evidence that they have met their *"minimum"* legal obligations – from there, I would leave it to the broader health and safety industry to devise how we are going to deliver on wider aspirations beyond the minimum.

To get us to this in point, I am going to:

1. Examine safety as a *"wicked problem"*, which will in part provide a framework to understand the inherent difficulty in using metrics to manage safety.

2. Provide an analysis of the legal framework and legal compliance. By way of forewarning, I should say that if we properly understood legal compliance and committed ourselves to achieving legal compliance, we would no longer have any need for aspirational objectives beyond legal compliance.

3. Provide a detailed analysis – at least from my legal/safety perspective – on the problems with workplace health and safety metrics. Again, by way of forewarning, I would say that my concern with the current application of metrics is not just that they do not do what they claim – often they are positively misleading, and therefore dangerous.

4. Describe a framework for proving safety.

Like most of my work, this book is set against the backdrop of my experience working within the Australian work health and safety regulatory framework. Nevertheless, I hope that there are elements and ideas in the book that go beyond the Australian legal framework, and indeed beyond Australia. In particular, the sections on Wicked Problems and Metrics should resonate beyond Australia and simple legal risk management. Hopefully also, the ideas in the last part of the book, *Framework for Proving Safety*, will provide food for thought for people testing ideas about work health and safety assurance from both a legal risk management and broader safety efficacy perspective.

I trust you will enjoy the journey through the next few pages as much as I did writing them.

Background

PART 2
A WORD ABOUT PROSECUTIONS AND CASE CITATIONS

By acting as a director of Quattro in name only, the offender failed to take reasonable steps to ensure that he was complying with his health and safety duty, including by implementing a SWMS for the site and making sure that the SWMS adequately controlled the risks to Quattro's workers on the site. The offender played an important role in subverting the policy underlying the Act, notwithstanding that his role was one at the lower end of the hierarchy. I am unable to make any finding on what, if any, benefit the offender received for agreeing to the appointment as a director of Quattro. I accept that he did not have as much to gain from the arrangement as others did.[12]

---

[12] *SafeWork NSW v Casella* [2023] NSWDC 503.

CASE STUDIES AND PROSECUTIONS

I have used a lot of case studies in this book, because I believe they are a compelling way to illustrate the points I am trying to make. However, case studies do have limitations.

The first type of *"case study"* I use, are my experiences from working with clients. Obviously, these observations are personal, subjective, and influenced by my own biases.

As far as possible, I have tried to place my experiences alongside published research, inquiries, reports, and cases. I have done this to try and illustrate that my experiences are consistent with published information about workplace accidents. I also believe this shows that the systemic failures of safety management we see when workplace accidents are publicly reported, are far more common and prevalent than we might think. Systemic failures in safety management can exist quite happily for many years without an accident.

The second type of case study I use are inquiries – most often major accident inquiries and coroners' reports.

These types of inquiries are very useful to help us understand safety management systems in practice, because typically, the inquiry has wide ranging terms of reference to understand *"why"* accidents happen and make recommendations about preventing future occurrences. An inquiry will have a broad remit, which allows it to go beyond the specific circumstances of an accident and look at safety management more holistically, including external influences such as regulators, economic pressure and so on.

In my experience, inquiries provide the best framework to understand safety management holistically and get a sense of how complex and interconnected safety management can be.

Finally, I have referred extensively to prosecutions under health and safety legislation.

These legal cases are helpful to understand the *"boundaries"* that apply to safety management and are, in my view, particularly important when we are trying to understand how to demonstrate or *"prove"* safety. How far do you have to go to provide safe systems of work?

However, reported prosecutions do have limitations in understanding safety management.

Prosecutions are not concerned with safety management per se. Prosecutions are concerned with the *"particulars"* of the charge against the defendant.

In a prosecution, the prosecutor alleges that a defendant has failed to do something – for example, failed to manage hazards in the workplace as far as *"reasonably practicable"*. The argument in a prosecution is not whether the defendant had safe systems of work, but rather, whether the prosecution can prove beyond a reasonable doubt the defendant failed to manage a particular hazard as far as reasonably practicable.

This structure creates some anomalies that people who are not familiar with the prosecution process find strange.

Legally, it is possible to have unsafe systems of work but to have managed a hazard *"as low as reasonably practicable"* in the context of a specific charge or a specific, particularised, breach of health and safety legislation. Reasonably practicable, is not the same as *"everything possible"* and just because something can be done which might improve safety, does not mean it has to be done.[13]

First, the law is quite clear; employers do not have to prevent all accidents. Employers only need take the steps set out in health and safety legislation. Complying with health and safety legislation is not always the same as preventing accident:

> *The Act does not require employers to ensure that accidents never happen. It requires them to take such steps as are practicable to provide and maintain a safe working environment.*[14]

Second, a defendant can breach their obligations even if their failure does not cause or contribute to an accident. Indeed, a defendant can breach their obligations even if there is no accident:

> *Crucially, the prosecution does not need to prove that the employer's breach 'caused' the accident, or that the taking of particular safety measures would have changed the course of events on the day in question. Put another way, the prosecution does not need to establish that the defendant employer should have anticipated the risk of events unfolding precisely as they did on the day of the fatal accident.*
>
> *As we have said, proof that the alleged breach caused the death (or injury) is not an element of the offence charged. On the contrary, as explained in the reasons which follow, the prosecution need only establish that:*

---

[13] *Baiada Poultry Pty Ltd v The Queen* [2012] HCA 14, [33] (**Baiada**).

[14] *Laing O'Rourke (BMC) Pty Ltd v Kirwin* [2011] WASCA 117, [31], citing with approval *Holmes v Re Spence & Co Pty Ltd* (1992) 5 VIR 119, 123 – 124.

> *(c)*[15] *there was a risk to employee health and safety;*
>
> *(d)   the measures identified as necessary would have eliminated or reduced the risk (as the case may be); and*
>
> *(e)   it was 'reasonably practicable' in the circumstances for the employer to have taken those measures.*[16]

Finally, prosecutions are limited to the allegations made against a defendant. This can result in a curious situation whereby an employer might be *"not guilty"* of the allegations against them, even though the case reveals failures of safety management which could otherwise give rise to a conviction.

For example, in the Cleary Brothers case[17] a worker was injured while unloading a truck at a waste collection facility. The worker slipped and fell into a pit which was about 1.8 metres deep. As result of the fall, the worker suffered serious head injuries, a broken rib, two broken wrists, as well as bruising and swelling.

The allegations against defendant were that they did not:

- install barriers to ensure a person could not fall into the pit; and
- ensure the floor next to the pit was clean and free of debris.

The Court found the defendant not guilty of the charges, saying:

> *I do not consider that it was reasonably practicable for the defendant to address the failings identified in the prosecutor's case. The prosecutor's case was limited to allegations that the defendant failed to provide an effective barrier and failed to ensure that the area was clean and free of debris. On the evidence before the Court, I am satisfied that the defendant has discharged its onus of proving that it was not reasonably practicable either to erect an effective barrier on the side of the pit catering for mechanically unloading vehicles or to ensure that the area beside the pit was always clean and free of debris so as to ensure that a person could not slip and fall.*[18]

However, at the end of the case the Court also made the following observation:

---

15   The seemingly incorrect reference to subparagraph (c) is taken directly from the case. It may be a typographical error.

16   *DPP v Vibro-Pile (Aust) Pty Ltd* [2016] VSCA 55, [5] – [6].

17   *Workcover Authority of New South Wales (Inspector Byer) v Cleary Bros (Bombo) Pty Ltd* [2001] NSWIRComm 278 (**Cleary Brothers**).

18   Cleary Brothers, [99].

> *Whilst it is not the position of the Court to specify what measures were required, it is possible that there were failings in effective supervision, adequate warnings or in the condition of the ground (even aside from the metal plates) that gave rise to the risk. These were not matters that were alleged as part of the prosecution.*[19]

This observation highlights one of the weaknesses inherent in prosecutions as a tool for safety improvement. The prosecution is limited to its charges – it is limited to its allegations about what might have been reasonably practicable.

While the prosecution could not prove it was reasonably practicable to erect the relevant barriers and keep the work area clean, there may have been other measures the employer could have taken to prevent the incident. However, the prosecution did not raise these *"other measures"* in the case.

Despite the limitations in different case studies, in their defence, they do offer useful insights into safety management. In my experience, the challenge is to focus on what can be learned and applied, rather than what is missing or might not make sense.

CASE CITATIONS

You can find the legal cases I have cited throughout this book at the Australasian Legal Information Institute website.[20] The website offers free access to Australian case law, legislation and other material, and while you are there, I encourage you to contribute to the site to help them continue their work.

For people who are not familiar with legal case citations, you will often see a reference to a number in square brackets, for example:

> *the phrase "reasonably practicable" means something narrower than "physically possible" or "feasible". [53]*

The number is a reference to the paragraph number which will help you find the referenced text most easily.

If you do have any trouble locating any of the references in the book, feel free to reach out to me and if I can, I will provide you with a copy of the material.

---

[19] Cleary Brothers, [100].
[20] www.austlii.edu.au.

Prosecutions and case citations

PART 3
WHAT IS SAFE?

Between 1992 and 1996 Esso employees worked 12 and a half million employee hours without a single lost time injury, a technical definition involving fatality, permanent disability or time lost from work. ... He pointed out that since these matters of 25 September 1998, at Longford over 1.7 million work hours have been completed without any lost time injury.

Esso also has received a number of safety awards. It has a five star rating award from the National Safety Council in 1991, APIA safety awards for 1994, 1995, 1996, 1999 and 2000, being the best safety performance of large companies, and the Fluor Daniel corporate tri-star award for 100,000 hours accident free in 1999. It also has other awards and commendable safety records including 100,000 mishap-free flying hours of helicopters to platforms. Credit there is properly given to Esso for its otherwise very good safety record.[21]

---

[21] *Director of Public Prosecutions v Esso Australia Pty Ltd* [2001] VSC 263, [29] – [30].

What is safe?

What is "*safe*"?

What do we mean when we use the term "*safe*" in the context of a workplace?

The Model WHS Act says:

> *The main object of this Act is to provide for a balanced and nationally consistent framework to secure the health and safety of workers and workplaces ..[22]*

However, I do not think many people would equate "*safe*" with a "*nationally consistent framework*".

Neither "*safe*" nor "*safety*" are defined in the Model WHS Act.

At one level, the "*safe*" question is problematic because it is so subjective. Most of us would understand the subjective nature of safety from being a passenger in a car. I recall being in South Korea for the World Speed Cubing Championships with my daughter in 2023. As we were travelling from the airport to our hotel when we first arrived in the country, our driver was doing 140 km an hour across a bridge with a posted speed limit of 80 km an hour.

I did not feel safe. The driver appeared completely unperturbed.

This may be an extreme example, but I imagine most people have from time to time felt, at least unsettled, as a passenger in a car while at the same time the driver is blissfully unaware of any concern.

It is almost certainly true that as individuals we can grow into a level of "*risk comfort*" over time, so that things that we initially perceived as dangerous or risky gradually become less concerning with familiarity. Objectively, the thing is no more or less safe – we have just become comfortable with it.

The subjective feeling of safety is not consistent. Again, to take a driving example, as we become familiar and comfortable with driving, we may appear complacent in our driving behaviour, almost on autopilot, but a "*near miss incident*" on the road – almost hitting another vehicle, or almost running off the road will instantaneously shift us into a state of heightened alertness or awareness – at least until we get comfortable again.

The same seems to be true in workplaces.

Individual workers will have different subjective experiences of "*safety*" at work, based on their individual work histories and experiences. And from time to time, workers will be jolted out of their

---

[22] https://www.safeworkaustralia.gov.au/sites/default/files/2022-06/model_whs_bill_-_14_april_2022.pdf

safety comfort zone by an incident or near miss, operating at higher levels of awareness and alertness until they get comfortable again.

The organisational challenge of what is safe is even more problematic. Organisations do not have a collective subjective sense of safety; we cannot amalgamate the feelings of the workforce to understand the collective sense of safety.

In an abstract to a recent article[23] the author sets out:

> *"The question 'what is safety?' and 'what is it that safety researchers study?' Are at the very core of safety research as an academic discipline. One might therefore assume that the discipline is based on clear answers to these questions, answers that are unanimously shared among the great majority of safety researchers. Strangely enough, this is not the case, and this lack of consensus is a major problem, ..."*

The author then canvasses various definitions of safety, including:

> *"the ability to succeed under expected and unexpected conditions alike, so that the number of intended and acceptable outcomes (in other words, every day activities) is as high as possible."* (Hollnagel).[24]

> *"an ability for a system to perform its intended purpose, while preventing harm to persons"* (Provan, Woods, Dekker and Rae).[25]

> *"freedom from losses defined as important to the system stakeholders"* (Leveson).[26]

> *"Safety is the ability to perform work in a varying and unpredictable workplace environment"* (Conklin).[27]

In the paper, the author argues that safety is the:

> *"... material, emotional and mental state that obtains when it is highly probable that all relevant positive values/valuables will be preserved for a desired duration, and the knowledge supporting this probability assessment is strong"[28]*

---

[23] Bjarne Vandekog, Safety is the preservation of value, https://doi.org/10.1016/j.jsr.2024.02.004 Journal of Safety Research, (**Vandekog**).

[24] Vandekog, p. 2.

[25] Vandekog, p. 3.

[26] Vandekog, p. 3.

[27] Vandekog, p. 3.

[28] Vandekog, p. 10.

Interestingly, none of these definitions of safety seem to make any allowance for accommodation of legal risk. Conversely, legal frameworks are generally quite happy to accommodate different methods of achieving safety outcomes. Indeed, as I will argue later in the book, the law does not care how you "*do*" safety so long as you can demonstrate whatever it is you do "*works*".

At the time of writing this book the health and safety industry appears to be a house very much divided against itself on the seemingly innocuous but apparently highly charged question of safety v high reliability v resilience engineering v safety I v safety II v (potentially) safety III v safety differently v human and organisational performance.

I am not going to even seek to dip a toe in the water of *"zero harm"* in this book.

Without seeking to fully traverse the terrain of the different or emergent *"safeties"*, I think I am right to say that the New View of safety promotes itself by identifying with the idea that safety does not means the absence of incidents, rather, safety means the presence of *"capacities"*.

But to return to the question of *"safe"*.

If I am wrong that an important distinction between New View safety, and what I will call for the sake of convenience only *"Traditional safety"*[29] is the distinction between safety being the absence of incidents or safety being the presence of capacities, and there are other ways of considering the question of what is *"safe"*, looking at these two camps will be sufficient for the purposes of this book and defining the problems of *"proving safety"*.

For a long time, in most organisations, safety was evidenced by a lack of accidents. And intuitively, this makes sense – if we are not having accidents, we must be safe, right? Can we say that the absence of accidents means that an organisation safe? With history as a guide, the answer to that question must be no.

The history of major accident events is filled with case examples of organisations that are ostensibly safe as evidenced by long periods without accidents. However, these apparently safe organisations have gone on to have devastating workplace accidents with subsequent inquiries finding significant gaps in the way that workplace health and

---

[29] Again, very loosely, for discussion purposes only, I use Traditional safety to mean safety ideas that pre-date or disagree with New View safety.

safety was managed. An especially notorious example of this history was the Deepwater Horizon disaster.[30]

On 20 April 2010, an explosion and fire overwhelmed the Deepwater Horizon drilling rig while it was undertaking deep water drilling of the Macondo well in the Gulf of Mexico.

The disaster resulted in 11 workers dying and untold environmental damage as millions of barrels of oil gushed into Gulf of Mexico.

The Deepwater Horizon rig had gone 7 years without a lost time injury – a widely accepted industry measure of safety performance. Yet, after the event, investigations illustrated that this apparently and objectively "*safe*" facility, was not:

> *The immediate causes of the Macondo well blowout can be traced to a series of identifiable mistakes made by BP, Halliburton, and Transocean that reveal such systematic failures in risk management that they place in doubt the safety culture of the entire industry.*[31]

Seven years without a lost time injury, yet a system of risk management that was so flawed it placed in doubt the "*safety culture of the entire industry*". Unfortunately, as we will see workplace accidents both before and since the Deepwater Horizon disaster are marked by similar difficulties – apparently good safety performance on the surface but fundamentally flawed safety management underneath.

But if the absence of accidents is not a reliable indicator of safety in an organisation, is the presence of capacities? As I understand the "*capacity*" position, it posits that safety should not be seen as an absence of negative events, but rather as the presence of capacities to make things go well, "*even under variable and sometimes messy conditions*".[32]

I think the jury is still out on whether we can "*measure*" these capacities[33], but even if we could reliably measure the capacities and even if we could be completely confident that these capacities create safety in a workplace, could we really rely on the presence of capacities as evidence that our workplace is safe? Surely the presence of capacities is

---

30 See: National Commission on the BP Deepwater Horizon Oil Spill and Offshore Drilling (2011). *Deep Water: The Gulf Oil Disaster and the Future of Offshore Drilling.* Report to the President (**Deepwater report**).

31 The Deepwater report, p. vii.

32 See for example Dekker, S.W.A. and Tooma, M. (2022), A capacity index to replace flawed incident-based metrics for worker safety. International Labour Review, 161: 375-393. https://doi.org/10.1111/ilr.12210 (**Due Diligence Index**).

33 See for example *Is a capacity index a good replacement for incident-count safety metrics?* from the Safety of Work Podcast https://safetyofwork.com/episodes/ep74-is-a-capacity-index-a-good-replacement-for-incident-count-safety-metrics.

only evidence that our workplace is safe for so long as we do not have accidents. And in that sense, is it any more reliable an indicator of safety than the absence of accidents?

If an organisation, confident in the presence of its capacities, had a catastrophic workplace accident that killed six people, could it have any more claim to being a "*safe*" workplace than an organisation that had gone 7 years without a lost time injury?

It seems to me to be a very difficult argument to make.

Logically, it seems that the presence of capacities is only a mark of safety while nothing goes wrong – in exactly the same way that the absence of accidents is only a marker of safety while nothing goes wrong.

And I do not think it is credible to argue that the presence of capacities is a better measure of safety because it makes accidents less likely to happen. I have worked with countless organisations over many years who measured safety using traditional methodologies and metrics – they did not think they would have an accident.

Hope is not a plan.

While appreciating that this is an entirely speculative and hypothetical proposition, I suspect that any major accident inquiry into an organisation that relied on the presence of capacity as a marker of safety would find the same types of systematic failures that has plagued major accident events for at least the past 30 years. It is likely that workplace health and safety management would be seen to fail in the same way as workplace health and safety management has been found to fail historically. And the presence of capacity is likely to become as discredited a measure of safety as the absence of accidents.

While I am going to be arguing that the legal framework of reasonably practicable, properly understood and overseen, provides at the very least a minimum foundation for understanding the state of workplace health and safety in an organisation, it is also problematic when we think about what we mean when we talk about a "*safe*" workplace.

If there has been a fatality in my workplace, but the regulator decides not to prosecute, can I argue my workplace is safe? Or, if I am prosecuted and found not guilty – the court determines I have done everything reasonably practicable to manage the hazards in my workplace – does that mean the workplace is safe?

On any reasonable interpretation you would have to think that the answer to that question would be no, So, it would seem then that whatever we do before an accident is no guarantee of safety, and that after an accident all we can say is "*we did the best we could*" and try to demonstrate that our workplace was as safe as possible.

In short, it appears that the problems inherent in *"proving safety"* are:

- organisations want to be able to demonstrate they are "*safe*";
- there is no legal definition of "*safe*";
- the health and safety industry has no agreed definition of "*safe*";
- the health and safety industry has no agreed set of principles to demonstrate that an organisation is "*safe*"; and
- all the processes and measures relied on to prove safety are unreliable and corruptible.

With history as a guide, it seems that none of our measures or philosophies describing what is safe in our own organisations are likely to stand up to the scrutiny that follows a major workplace catastrophe.

Given these difficulties, perhaps a starting point (at least) might be an understanding of the legal framework so as to consider what the legal compliance obligations really look like and see how far that framework might satisfy an organisation's need to evidence safety.

What is safe?

PART 4
THE LEGAL FRAMEWORK

The words "reasonably practicable" have, somewhat surprisingly, been the subject of much judicial consideration. It is surprising because the words "reasonably practicable" are ordinary words bearing their ordinary meaning. And the question whether a measure is or is not reasonably practicable is one which requires no more than the making of a value judgment in the light of all the facts.[34]

---

[34] *Slivak v Lurgi (Australia) Pty Ltd* [2001] HCA 6, [53], per Gaudron J (**Slivak**).

The legal framework

As I have already suggested, legal obligations are often described by the health and safety industry as the *"minimum"* expectation. Unfortunately, however, I think this demonstrates a misunderstanding of what compliance with legal obligations means, and the workplace health and safety benefits an organisation could achieve if they properly understood legal obligations and compliance, and dedicated energy to meeting those standards.

I think historically, the health and safety industry has equated the *"completion of paperwork"* with *"legal compliance"* – if I fill out the form, I am legally compliant.

This is a misconception.

Cases considering prosecutions under work health and safety legislation have always called out the *"tick and flick"* approach to workplace health and safety management.

I think if there was greater recognition about what legal compliance with workplace health and safety obligations looked like, then there would be less reluctant to pursue legal compliance as a legitimate strategy for creating better workplace safety.

It does seem to me that in some cases a disdain for legal obligations amongst some in the health and safety industry has seen us embark on strategies which ignore legal compliance (or at least do not consider it) and do not add much value in terms of practical safety outcomes.

Part of the problem I think arises from mistaking *"evidencing activity"* with *"legal compliance"*. They are not the same thing:

> *The prosecution then indicated that such a document is to be distributed and a record made as to who received the document. This is of course desirable but what would it have achieved against a background of constant verbal reinforcement? Recording who received the document had not been carried out in the past although there was a universal awareness of the document by the employees and former employees ...*[35]

Compliance with legal obligations can be evidenced without paperwork, and safety documentation is not, of itself, evidence of legal compliance. Indeed, there are examples of organisations that have been able to demonstrate they have met their legal obligations without any documented safety management systems at all.[36]

---

[35] *Moore v SD Tillett Memorials Pty Ltd* [2002] SAIRC 47, [82] (**SD Tillett**).
[36] See for example: SD Tillett and *Safe Work NSW v Wollongong Glass P/L* [2016] NSWDC 58 (**Wollongong Glass**).

Early in the book I commented about the apparent disharmony in workplace health and safety between Traditional and New Views of safety. While each tradition has its own academic and intellectual backgrounds, essentially it seems to me they are arguments about how organisations should "*do*" safety.

From a legal risk management perspective this is largely a moot point. Relevantly, there is nothing inherent or intrinsic in either the Traditional or the New View of safety that makes them better or worse for legal risk management. Moreover, courts do not care how you "*do*" safety. Courts are only interested in your ability to demonstrate that your approach to workplace health and safety management "*works*". Was your system to manage workplace health and safety sufficient to meet your legal obligations?

Some of the basics of legal compliance can be illustrated by comparing two cases; Wollongong Glass and the Desiya case.[37]

DESIYA

In the Desiya case, a worker was killed when they were hit by a truck while walking in a grain receival yard.

The formal, documented systems of work to manage the work health and safety risks generally, were limited at best. Relevantly:

- there were no documented procedures for training drivers and no formal training processes;
- training and assessment of drivers was provided on the job;
- yard managers and yard supervisors provided on-the-job training, and while they were experienced and competent in the operation of the trucks, for a period of 9 months (during which the accident occurred) they were not licensed to drive relevant heavy vehicles;
- the competence of trainers and trainees had not been assessed against any objective criteria;
- no risk assessment had been done in relation to vehicle movement and vehicle/people interaction;
- there was no adequate traffic management on site, with the only traffic management being enforcement of a 10 km an hour speed limit; and
- at the time of the accident there were no documented procedures in place to separate moving plant from pedestrians.

---

[37] *Inspector Shepherd v Desiya Pty Ltd* [2013] NSWIRComm 9 (**Desiya**).

The legal framework

Health and safety management on site, as described by one of the managers, was referred to by the court as *"largely practical, observational and 'hands-on' based rather than documented or theory based"*[38]

In its findings the court described that:

> *"There was no effective system at the premises to ensure vehicles and pedestrians interacted safely"* [49]

and

> *"whatever system there was depended largely on workers exercising care when driving vehicles and alighting from vehicles. That was clearly inadequate in circumstances where there might be up to 50 employees on site and a large number of heavy vehicles and plant." [50]*

The court found that the company was aware of the relevant risks:

> *"the defendants were clearly aware of the risk of pedestrians being struck by moving vehicles struck by a moving vehicle..."*[39]

However, there was no evidence of:

- appropriate systems to manage the risk of pedestrians being hit by moving vehicles in the workplace; or
- that workers were aware of the controls to manage the risks of pedestrians being hit by moving vehicles in the workplace; or
- the extent to which workers were aware of or complied with any controls to manage the risks of pedestrians being hit by moving vehicles.

In the end, the company was convicted of breaches of its workplace health and safety obligations.

WOLLONGONG GLASS

The Wollongong Glass case involved a worker who was killed helping another worker to lean sheets of glass away from an A – frame so that the other worker could get to one of the sheets at the back of the stack.

The glass sheets were 2.3 m high by 2.1 m wide and weighed approximately 80 kg each.

---

[38] Desiya, [34].
[39] Desiya, [56].

While moving the sheets of glass, the cumulative weight of the glass became too much, and they fell causing the worker fatal head injuries.

The court found that:

> *"It was common ground that the defendant had in place a system of work at the time of the incident. It was not reduced to writing. It was implemented through verbal direction and on-the-job training and enforced by supervision. There were mechanical means available to workers for use in handling and lifting glass sheets, i.e. the crane."[40] [65]*

The court also observed that reducing the work health and safety requirements for handling the glass, by developing a safe work method statement, seemed to be an integral part of the prosecution case.[41]

The court dismissed the idea that a safe work method statement was a reasonably practicable measure that the company should have taken. The court observed that a safe work method statement was only a requirement under the relevant regulations for *"high risk construction work"*, and handling the glass was not high-risk construction work. Moreover, while the company did adopt a safe work method statement after the fatality the court noted that several workers could not read it.[42]

The court found that the effect of the evidence in the case was that:

- workers were aware that it was unsafe for the deceased worker to do what they did[43]; and
- none of the witnesses had ever seen another worker do what the deceased had done.[44]

Ultimately, the court found:

> *"it was not reasonably practicable to prohibit the workers from attempting to support multiple glass sheets by hand, because it was not a practice adopted in the factory, it was contrary to the instructions given to the workers by the defendant and thereby it was not reasonably foreseeable. The precise mechanism of the incident occurred by reason of the deceased acting irrationally and by both the deceased and [the other worker] acting against instructions and with a significant disregard for safety. That sort of circumstances also not reasonably foreseeable."[45]*

---

40 Wollongong Glass, [65].
41 Wollongong Glass, [66] – [67].
42 Wollongong Glass, [96] – [98].
43 Wollongong Glass, [103].
44 Wollongong Glass, [104].
45 Wollongong Glass, [109].

The legal framework

In this case, Wollongong Glass was acquitted of the charges against it.

There is one further case that I think is useful to help illustrate the role of work, knowledge, and systems of work in the context of the legal framework.

In the Hunter Quarries case[46] a worker was operating an excavator on an uneven slope at the northern end of the quarry. The excavator rolled over and the worker was crushed inside the cabin. He died as a result of injuries sustained in the accident.

The company was charged with breaches of health and safety legislation and pleaded not guilty, meaning that the court undertook a thorough examination of the systems that were in place to manage the health and safety risks associated with the business.

Relevantly:

- the area where the excavator had been operating and had rolled over was a *"no go"* zone;
- the area was bunded off, but the excavator had been driven across the bund separating the haul road from the no-go area, flattening the bund in the process;
- the worker was not instructed to take the excavator into the no-go zone to do any work;
- there was no reason for the excavator to be in that no-go zone;
- there was no reason why anyone at the quarry would have known that the worker was working in the no-go zone;
- in operating the excavator on the rocky slope, the worker breached a well-known rule in the quarry that no-one was to cross a bund; and
- the worker was operating the excavator in a manner contrary to how he had been trained, which was to operate the excavator on a level surface, not across a slope, and with the boom close to the body of the excavator.

The prosecutor submitted that the safety documentation at the quarry was a confused and chaotic system, and the court noted that the defendant *"could not produce a complete and seamless collection of written safety documents"*. However, the court went on to say that:

> *"... all the safety documentation in the world is of little use*
> *unless workers are trained in matters of safety, and safe*

---

[46]   *Orr v Hunter Quarries Pty Limited* [2019] NSWDC 634 (**Hunter Quarries**.)

> *working practices are then constantly observed and enforced."*[47]

The court went on to reference various earlier decisions noting that not all systems of work need to be documented, and that the absence of a written procedure is not conclusive evidence of a failure to have safe systems of work.[48]

The court found that the worker had operated contrary to the known rules of the quarry, and while not all the procedures or rules were appropriately documented in the safety management system, the safety rules were implemented, observed and enforced within the quarry by oral instructions and observations.[49]

What these cases (Wollongong Glass, Desiya and Hunter Quarries) clearly demonstrate in my view, is the importance of worker understanding.

Where a business can establish that workers understand the workplace health and safety hazards associated with their work, and that there were appropriate controls that the workers understood, and usually applied, then the business is well-placed to build an argument that they had met their obligations to do everything reasonably practicable. This position appears to hold true even when the business has no documented, or poorly documented, workplace health and safety management systems.

At its core, legal compliance is about ensuring an organisation has *"proper"* systems to manage the health and safety hazards arising from their business activities and adequate *"supervision"* to ensure that those systems are in place and effective. I cannot help but think that any organisation with a consistent, critical focus on those two factors and a good understanding of systems, their implementation and efficacy would achieve good workplace health and safety outcomes – not just legal compliance.

Having said that, I think there are areas where legal risk management (as opposed to legal compliance) can conflict with what the health and safety industry would regard as good safety practice. One of those is the protection of information through legal professional privilege.

---

[47] Hunter Quarries, [285]

[48] Hunter Quarries, [287]. See also *Morrison v Milner and Baldwin (No. 2)* [2009] NSWIRComm 191; *Genner Constructions Pty Ltd v WorkCover Authority of New South Wales (Inspector Guillarte)* [2001] NSWIRComm 267; *Inspector Kilpatrick v Jae My Pty Limited* [2004] NSWIRComm 109; *WorkCover Authority of New South Wales (Inspector Patton) v Fletcher Constructions Australia Ltd* [2002] NSWIRComm 316.

[49] Hunter Quarries, [288].

While I think legal professional privilege is an important legal right, and one that organisations do need to seriously consider in the wake workplace accident having regard to the significance of penalties under Australia's work health and safety regime, it is not, strictly speaking relevant to the question of proving safety. However, it is a topic that I often get asked about and I have included a short summary of the fundamentals of legal professional privilege as an annexure to this book.

SUMMARY OF THE LEGAL FRAMEWORK

An understanding of the legal framework – particularly the concepts of *"reasonably practicable"* and *"due diligence"* under Australian health and safety legislation is important to help make sense of my comments about existing workplace health and safety metrics and the arguments I want to make that workplace health and safety metrics are not useful when it comes to defending legal proceedings under health and safety legislation.

While Australian health and safety legislation is voluminous and replete with technical specifications, including accompanying *"referenced"* codes of practice[50] the legal liability framework at one level is very linear and simple. Organisations are expected to:

- identify the activities they perform as part of their business or undertaking;
- identify any technical legal requirements arising from those activities – for example if the business operates forklifts, then the drivers of those forklifts must have a high-risk work licence to operate them;
- identify any hazards arising from the activities;

---

[50] Ordinarily in prosecutions under work health and safety legislation if the prosecution wants to introduce evidence in the case, then it needs to be done in accordance with the "*rules of evidence*" as they apply in the relevant jurisdiction. However, there are specific provisions in work health and safety legislation that gives special status to codes of practice. Under work health and safety legislation, codes of practice approved in accordance with the relevant health and safety legislation are automatically admissible as evidence of what it was reasonably practicable to do to manage a particular hazard. That does not mean that a defendant is legally obliged to comply with the code of practice, and a defendant can demonstrate it has met its obligations under work health and safety legislation other than by complying with the practice – but the code of practice is automatically available to the prosecutor as evidence of what the defendant *could* have done. By contrast, if the prosecution wanted to introduce evidence that it was normal industry practice to make new employees on a construction site wear a green helmet to identify them as new employees, something that is not covered by a code of practice, the prosecution would have to call witnesses to give that evidence to try and establish it as an industry practice.

- risk assess those hazards;
- develop controls to manage the hazards;
- ensure those controls are implemented, enforced and effective; and
- have an overarching system of review and improvement.

A significant challenge for workplace health and safety in the context of this framework is reaching consensus on how we do it and how we evidence it. It seems a trite thing to say that organisations need to ensure that controls to manage workplace hazards are implemented, enforced and effective but when it comes to achieving that outcome, we can end up having significant arguments about how that should be achieved. Something as apparently straightforward as going out and having conversations with workers to confirm if control mechanisms are in place has, over the years, generated enormous amounts of controversy, not to mention a myriad of commercially available "*solutions*".

On top of the challenge of working out how to achieve the objectives of the framework described above, whatever actions we take always seem to generate mountains of administration and bureaucracy which, in my experience at least, often has the perverse effect of undermining the integrity and efficacy of the safety initiative. And oddly, in my view, very often the way that we design and implement measures to ensure controls are implemented, enforced and effective do not seem to have any useful connection, to or understanding of, the principles underpinning the legal framework we are trying to evidence.

Courts have interpreted health and safety legislation over the years, providing a detailed and nuanced description of the elements that need to be considered when passing judgement on the legal liability framework.

Two of the key terms under Australian health and safety legislation central to questions of liability are "*reasonably practicable*" and "*due diligence*". I have described both terms and their interpretation by the courts below.

When reviewing the issues of reasonable practicability and due diligence, it is worth asking yourself two questions. First, whether your existing workplace health and safety reporting frameworks, metrics and information give you any insight about the extent to which your organisation is meeting the expectations created by the principles of reasonably practicable and due diligence.

A second important question is whether, or to what extent, compliance with these elements – properly understood – would benefit health and safety in your workplace.

The legal framework

REASONABLY PRACTICABLE

Reasonably practicable is the primary duty described in work health and safety legislation in many jurisdictions around the world. Reasonably practicable is certainly the cornerstone of health and safety legislation in Australia.

From the perspective of the courts and legal practitioners who specialise in the area, the principles of reasonably practicable are well-known and have been clearly enunciated by the courts for many, many years. Of course, courts and lawyers have the significant advantage of addressing the question of what was, or what was not, reasonably practicable after the event with the 20/20 vision accorded by hindsight. Organisations, their leadership, their workplace health and safety advisors, and workers have the rather more complex task of approaching the question of reasonably practicable with the far less perfect handicap of foresight - a challenge not lost on the courts:

> *The Act does not require employers to ensure that accidents never happen. It requires them to take such steps as are practicable to provide and maintain a safe working environment. The courts will best assist the attainment of this end by looking at the facts of each case as practical people would look at them: not with the benefit of hindsight, nor with the wisdom of Solomon, but nevertheless remembering that one of the chief responsibilities of all employers is the safety of those who work for them.*[51]

Despite our best efforts to avoid the influence of hindsight it is omnipresent, particularly in the cold light of day following a workplace fatality. What becomes blindingly obvious after the event is often obscured by the multitude of workplace hazards, distractions and day-to-day operations demanding the attention of organisations and their leadership.

Notwithstanding its centrality, the principles of reasonably practicable as defined by the courts are often a mystery to organisations and their health and safety advisors. Indeed, some of the nonsense that is peddled as being descriptive of reasonably practicable – particularly by nonlawyers – is especially troubling.

In Australia at least, reasonably practicable is a defined term in legislation. In the case of the Model WHS Act, it is defined as follows:

---

[51]   *Holmes v RE Spence & Co Pty Ltd* (1992) VIR 119, 123 – 124.

> *reasonably practicable*, in relation to a duty to ensure health and safety, means that which is, or was at a particular time, reasonably able to be done in relation to ensuring health and safety, taking into account and weighing up all relevant matters including –
>
> (a)   the likelihood of the hazard or the risk concerned occurring; and
>
> (b)   the degree of harm that might result from the hazard or the risk; and
>
> (c)   what the person concerned knows, or ought reasonably to know, about —
>
>   (i)   the hazard or the risk; and
>
>   (ii)   ways of eliminating or minimising the risk; and
>
> (d)   the availability and suitability of ways to eliminate or minimise the risk; and
>
> (e)   after assessing the extent of the risk and the available ways of eliminating or minimising the risk, the cost associated with available ways of eliminating or minimising the risk, including whether the cost is grossly disproportionate to the risk.

However, like many definitions or other provisions contained in legislation, those provisions are, necessarily, subject to judicial interpretation. For example:

- Where the definition of reasonably practicable says we must weigh up all relevant matters *"including"* (i.e., not limited to) what else do we have to consider?
- Having weighed up the *"relevant matters"* (or at least those we could think of), how do we determine whether something is *"reasonably able to be done"*?
- Just because something could be physically done, is that the same as *"reasonably able"* to be done?
- What considerations do we need to apply in trying to work out whether somebody *"ought reasonably to know about"* a hazard?
- When is a control available and suitable to eliminate or minimise the risk?
- When is a cost *"grossly disproportionate"*?

These are all questions guided by the facts in the circumstances of each case and judicial precedent.

THE PRINCIPLES

As mentioned earlier, while not expressly referenced in the Model WHS Act, the principles underpinning reasonably practicable as defined by the courts are well-known and long enunciated, and I have set out a summary below.

Many of the cases cited below which establish the principles of reasonably practicable, and which are cited with approval in recent cases, are decades old. However, they continue to be cited as authority and recent decisions (at the time of writing) continue to uphold the principles described below.

An objective test

The state of knowledge applied to the definition of reasonably practicable is objective.

It is the knowledge of persons generally engaged in a relevant field of activity and should not be assessed by reference to the *actual* knowledge of a specific defendant in particular circumstances.[52]

So, if I am a builder and I have a workplace accident in my business the question of what I knew or ought to have known about the hazards and risks leading to that accident is not answered by my personal, subjective understanding of the hazards and risks, but rather by what a person operating in the building industry generally ought to have known.

I was involved in a prosecution of a company and a manager following a fall from height fatality during construction work. At the time, legislation in Western Australia required that if a person was working in circumstances where there was a risk of falling 3m or more, edge protection had to be in place. My client had mistakenly understood this requirement to mean that if you were working more than 3m away from an edge, no fall protection was required.

My client's mistaken belief was not a defensible position.

How do courts and tribunals establish the *"general"* state of knowledge that a person should have?

In most cases, the evidence of the general state of knowledge is reasonably straightforward. It includes factors such as:

- legislation (as in the case of my client);
- material published by regulators, such as incident alerts, guidance notes or codes of practice; and

---

[52]   *Laing O'Rourke (BMC) Pty Ltd v Kirwin* [2011] WASCA 117, [33].

- published standards such as Australian Standards or ISO standards.

Sometimes, in the absence of any documentary evidence it will be necessary for parties to call expert witnesses to speak to what is *"usual"* industry practice.

For example, in the case, of Anthony Robert Russell[53] a supervisor had directed an apprentice to screw a tech screw into a copper reticulation pipe to see if it was redundant. The supervisor's thinking was, because the tech screw had a rubber seal at the top, if there was water in the reticulation pipe the apprentice could simply screw it in all the way and the rubber seal would stop the water flowing until it could be dealt with. Unfortunately, there was a misunderstanding between the apprentice and the supervisor as to which *"pipe"* needed to be dealt with, and the apprentice ended up screwing the tech screw into a 11,000 V high-voltage mains electrical conduit resulting in an explosion caused by a phase to earth flashover which threw the apprentice out of the trench where he was operating.

As part of the decision the court found that drilling into a water pipe in this way was not standard procedure for the company, *or in the industry generally.*

Another very common way that Courts and tribunals can determine the general state of knowledge in relation to work practices is by looking at the organisation's own policies and procedures. If an organisation has a policy or procedure that describes how work is going to be performed, then that is objective knowledge as to what was reasonably practicable.

As a general principle, courts will almost always find that it was reasonably practicable for an organisation to implement and enforce their own documented procedures.

Control, supervision, and management

The reasonably practicable requirement applies to matters which are within the power of the of an organisation to control, supervise and manage.[54]

In the Slivak decision, a worker was injured when he fell from a fume extraction system during construction. The worker was employed by a subcontractor.

---

[53] Magistrates Court of Western Australia – Perth, charge number PE 76692/14, 2 May 2014.

[54] Slivak, [37].

The legal framework

The tower forming the fume extraction system was 25 metres high. It was designed so that air would rise through the tower through a filter system, and flow out through a funnel at its bottom. The filter system was located about 15 metres from the ground and comprised four "*cell plates*", each about 6 mm thick and weighing about one tonne each. The cell plates were set up in a 2 x 2 formation on a support structure.

The support structure was made up of steel supports welded to the inside of the tower at various heights and a "*cross frame*" comprising two steel beams crossing at right angles. Each cell plate rested on the steel supports on two adjacent sides and on a cross frame on its other two sides. Three corners of each cell plate were cut off at a 45-degree angle 200 mm from the corner, with the remaining intact corner designed to sit near a corner of the tower. The design required that the cell plates were welded to the support structure to fix them in place.

While two workers were trying to weld a cell plate into position, they decided it needed to be moved about 25 – 30 mm, but while doing so the cell plate fell and both workers fell with it.

The evidence in the case demonstrated that:

- as designed, a cell plate could not become unsupported on both sides and fall; and
- the support structure had not been erected completely square.

The case turned on the question of whether it was reasonable for the designer of the fume extraction system to expect that the structure would be erected within the specific design tolerances or whether the designer needed to warn the constructor about the need to comply with design specifications and anticipate a system of unsafe work.

In the end, the court found that the designer held no such obligations stating:

> *The [so far as is reasonably practicable] requirement applies to matters which are within the power of the designer to perform or check, such as ascertaining what use the structure will be put to, what loads it will experience when being built and the nature of the location in which it is to be erected. This is in contrast to the matters that would be forced within the ambit of this requirement were the submissions for the appellants accepted; for then a designer would be required to take account of factors outside the power of the designer to control, supervise or*

> *manage, such as the procedures to be adopted during construction.*[55]

Not everything possible

Reasonably practicable means something narrower than physically possible or feasible.[56]:

> *The reasonably practicable duty does not require a duty holder to take every possible step that could be taken. The duty requires taking such steps as are reasonably practicable for the duty holder to achieve the provision and maintenance of a safe working environment. Bare demonstration that a step might have had some effect on the safety of a working environment does not, without more, demonstrate a breach of the duty.*[57]

It is also the case that employers are not expected to prevent all accidents:

> *The Act does not require employers to ensure that accidents never happen. It requires them to take such steps as are practicable to provide and maintain a safe working environment. The courts will best assist the attainment of this end by looking at the facts of each case as practical people would look at them: not with the benefit of hindsight, nor with the wisdom of Solomon, but nevertheless remembering that one of the chief responsibilities of all employers is the safety of those who work for them.*[58]

The limits of practicability was a question explored in the Sanders decision.[59] In the case a bricklayer working for a subcontractor on the Perth Stadium construction project suffered serious injuries when he single-handedly began to remove two overhead steel purlins that were in the way when he was building a wall. One of the discussions in the case was the extent to which the principal should have provided training to the subcontractor about workplace health and safety hazards associated with the work. In that context, the court observed:

> *Pursuant to its contract, NeoWest had autonomy in how it was to complete the works and it was the appropriate body to provide the training and induction within its specialised*

---

55   Slivak, [37].
56   Slivak, [53].
57   *Baiada Poultry Pty Ltd v R* (2012) 246 CLR 92, [15], [33] and [38] (**Baiada**).
58   *Holmes v RE Spence & Co Pty Ltd* (1992) 5 VIR 119, 123-4. See also *Laing O'Rouke (BMC) Pty Ltd v Kirwin* [2011] WASCA 117.
59   *Sanders v Multiplex Engineering & Infrastructure Pty Ltd* [2022] WADC 31 (**Sanders**).

> *area and to specify the methods to be used in performing the tasks required of its workers. It would not have been reasonably practicable, or indeed wise, for the first defendant to impinge on NeoWest's training and induction of its own employees as to the proper and safe method of completing the works within its scope of works and area of expertise and specialised knowledge, possibly to override or even contradict that training and induction. Each individual trade's expertise and specialist knowledge was the very reason why the first defendant engaged subcontractors to perform the various works in the first place, rather than complete them itself.[60]*

This limited (although still very onerous) obligation is consistent with a social approach to managing wicked problems. As I argue later in the book, you cannot solve wicked problems – we cannot solve safety. All we can do is "*tame*" the problem of safety – do the best we can.

The notion of reasonably practicable, and the recognition that we do not have to do everything physically possible to manage workplace health and safety hazards, creates a boundary around our obligations. There are "*limits to the practicability*" of what organisations can do to manage workplace health and safety risks.

Foreseeability of risk

The reasonably practicable duty requires knowledge of the risk emanating from the activities of the defendant and foreseeability of the risk to persons from the activities of the business is an element of this question of knowledge. It would not generally be practicable to take measures to guard against a risk to safety that was not reasonably foreseeable.[61]

> *The unforeseeable behaviour of a disobedient worker may well lead to the happening of an event that could not be reasonably foreseen and therefore was not reasonably practicable to guard against.[62]*

The concept of foreseeability often comes up in prosecutions as arguments about the foreseeability that a worker would not comply with the organisation's safety requirements.

---

[60] Sanders, [324].
[61] *Genner Constructions Pty Ltd v WorkCover Authority of New South Wales* [2001] NSWIRComm 267, [68] (**Genner**).
[62] *WorkCover Authority of New South Wales v Kirk Group Holdings Pty Ltd* (2004) 135 IR 166, [129]

In the Genner case, a worker was killed when they were hit by a truck that was leaving the work site after the truck had delivered a load of gravel. The company's usual practice for the movement of vehicles on and off the worksite was for them to enter and leave with the normal flow of traffic. However, on the day of the accident, a subcontracted, self-employed grader operator decided to change the usual practice by directing the vehicles using "*industry understood*" hand signals to cross the traffic flow. The reason he changed the usual practice was because of high wind that was causing spray from the gravel when the trucks tipped their loads.

The company was convicted at first instance, and part of the company's argument on appeal was that the accident occurred because of an "*inadvertent or casual failure*" on the part of the subcontractor and the deceased worker to observe the company's safe system of work.

A significant part of the argument was whether the company had provided adequate training and instruction to the deceased worker, Mr Ingram, who was a leading hand employed by the company.

Relevant case law sets out that:

> *it may not be practicable to guard against a detriment to safety occasioned by an appropriately trained and instructed employee departing from a known procedure.*

and

> *There are limits to the degree of instruction which can be expected to be provided to an experienced employee.*[63]

The prosecution had argued that if adequate instructions had been given to either Mr Ingram or the subcontractor about the necessary safety steps if trucks were bought onto site against the flow of traffic, then much of the risk would have been eliminated.

The company argued that Mr Ingram had received appropriate training.

> *The appellant pointed to the evidence of Mr Genner to the effect that he had provided regular "on-the-job" training and instruction to Mr Ingram over many years. The evidence of Mr Genner was that this training encompassed issues of safety, including methods of directing vehicles entering and leaving worksites. Inspector Chadwick of the WorkCover Authority and Mr Johnson, an expert called by the appellant in the proceedings at first instance, agreed*

---

[63]   *Inspector Orr v Perilya Broken Hill Limited* [2018] NSWDC 28, [68].

> *that "on-the-job" training can be a very effective method of training workers.[64]*

The court accepted that in some circumstances on-the-job training may be effective and appropriate, however went on to note:

> *The extent and standard of training provided by employers to their employees to ensure satisfaction with the requirements of the Act will depend upon the nature of, and circumstances under which, work is performed. It will not, therefore, necessarily require the provision of classroom-based instruction or the provision of substantial work manuals. However, in all cases, adequate training will necessarily involve the provision of such information and instruction as will fully equip employees to safely perform work which they are expected to undertake, including the provision of training as to all contingencies arising out of or relating to the performance of such work. In short, the employer must educate the employee to deal with the full range of circumstances which may arise in the performance of work, including eventualities which are more unusual in character. Such education should involve processes designed to ensure that employees have fully understood the training afforded them (and re-training of employees, where necessary, to ensure the continued sufficiency of such education).[65]*

Ultimately, however, the argument that Mr Ingram had received adequate training was rejected by the court:

> *In this case, we are satisfied beyond reasonable doubt that the training provided to Mr Ingram was not adequate to ensure he was not exposed to risks to his health and safety in relation to the control of vehicular movements onto and off the worksite. The training received by Mr Ingram over the years he had been working for the appellant was solely informal, ad hoc training and provided directly by Mr Genner. The training was not documented and the appellant's procedure for controlling vehicles entering and leaving a worksite were not recorded or refined. In our view, it is proper to conclude there was not sufficiently systematic or comprehensive training so as to ensure that Mr Ingram, who was left in control of the worksite, was*

---

64   Genner, [57].
65   Genner, [58].

> *sufficiently trained to react to changing circumstances and*
> *at the same time to ensure the site remained safe.*[66]

As described earlier, a different conclusion was reached in the Wollongong Glass case. In the Wollongong Glass case, a worker was killed trying manually move sheets of glass on a trolley, rather than use an overhead crane.

One of the interesting things about the Wollongong Glass case is that the safety management systems were not documented, with the court noting that the company did have a system of work in place at the time of the incident, but he was not reduced to writing and it was implemented through verbal directions and on-the-job training enforced by supervision.

The prosecution described the systems of work as *"'informal', 'ad hoc' and involving the exercise of a worker's discretion based on their experience..."*[67]

As discussed earlier, one of the key arguments by the prosecution was that the systems of work for managing the glass ought to have been reduced to a safe work method statement. This position was rejected by the court for several reasons, including:

- a safe work method statement was only required for high-risk construction work, and this work was not high risk construction work;

- workers were confident within the meaning of the relevant regulations, as they had acquired knowledge and skills to carry out their tasks through training, qualification or experience – notwithstanding the lack of written records;

- safe work method statement might provide evidence that there is a safe work procedure, but it does not follow that workers will have been trained in the content of the safe work method statement or that they would comply with it. The workers involved in the incident were both *"considered to be good workers"*, but neither of them could read the safe work method statement was eventually adopted after the accident; and

- the workers were adequately trained to a system of oral instruction and on-the-job training, and that training was enforced by adequate supervision.[68].

---

66   Genner, [59].
67   Wollongong Glass, [66].
68   Wollongong Glass, [95] – [99]

The legal framework

All the workers called as witnesses in the Wollongong Glass case gave evidence about the systems of work to move the glass, and that evidence was all consistent. They also all gave evidence that they had never seen a person do what the worker was attempting to do before the fatal accident. Each supervisor gave evidence that if they had seen the worker doing what he was doing, they would have intervened to stop the conduct because it was unsafe.

The evidence in the case established that the company had a safe system of work for managing the glass on the trolleys, that all the workers understood that system, that none of the workers would have done what the deceased worker did, and that all the workers understood what the deceased worker did was unsafe:

> *It was not reasonably practicable to prohibit the workers from attempting to support multiple glass sheets by hand, because it was not a practice adopted in the factory, it was contrary to the instructions given to the workers by the defendant and thereby it was not reasonably foreseeable. The precise mechanism of the incident occurred by reason of the deceased acting irrationally and by both the deceased and Mr Pham acting against instructions and with a significant disregard for safety. That set of circumstances was also not reasonably foreseeable.[69]*

Obligations to careless workers

One of the tensions in understanding reasonably practicable is that while it may not always be possible to foresee that a worker may not comply with the safe systems of work that apply to them, nevertheless, companies must recognise that workers will not always comply with the organisation's safety management systems and factor that reality into their work health and safety management systems.

A duty holder must have regard not only for the ideal worker but also for one who is careless, inattentive, or inadvertent.[70]

If there is a foreseeable risk arising from a worker's negligence in carrying out their duties and this must be taken into account.[71]

It may not always possible to foresee various acts of inadvertence by workers, but duty holders must conduct operations on the basis that such acts will occur, and they must be guarded against to the fullest extent practicable.

---

[69] Wollongong Glass, [109].
[70] *Dunlop Rubber Australia Ltd* (1952) 87 CLR 313, 320.
[71] *Smith v Broken Hill Pty Ltd* (1957) 97 CLR 337, 343.

One of the matters PCBUs must recognise and plan for is the inevitability of human error ranging from inadvertence, inattention or haste through to foolish disregard of personal safety and deliberate non-compliance with safe systems of work.[72]:

It is also important to recognise that it is not just workers who behave "*unacceptably*" that need to be considered in this context. In some instances, it is workers operating with the best intentions that may be problematic in the context of workplace health and safety.

The Montara Commission of Inquiry[73] concerned a blowout on an offshore drilling rig, the West Atlas, on 21 August 2009. Although there were no fatalities arising from the incident, the event was the third largest oil spill in Australia's history and was subject to a commission of inquiry.

One of the factors identified in the Montara Report was that management did not give enough credit to the fact that workers might take shortcuts – not because of inadvertence or inattention – but rather because of their desire to do the job quickly and profitably:

> *In this regard, the Inquiry notes that Mr Jacob gave evidence to the effect that he found it hard to credit that PTTEPAA personnel might pursue time and cost savings to the detriment of proper procedures. He thought that the Project Manager and CEO would share his view. Indeed, he stated:*

> > *...I don't think anybody in the organisation would credit that things would be done to the detriment of safety for the benefit of cost.[74]*

From a legal risk management perspective these types of deficiencies, and we will explore this further when we look at the case studies dealing with due diligence, can be used to illustrate a lack of organisational oversight and assurance:

> *PTTEPAA's supervisory systems were not really directed toward achieving effective quality assurance. Later in his evidence Mr Jacob frankly accepted that the supervisory deficiencies infected the entire organisation:*

---

[72] *R v Commercial Industrial Construction Group Pty Ltd* (2006) 14 VR 321, [49] and *Director of Public Prosecutions v JCS Fabrications Pty Ltd and JMAL Group Pty Ltd* [2019] VSCA 50, [51].

[73] Inquiry Website: https://www.industry.gov.au/publications/montara-commission-inquiry; Inquiry Report: Borthwick, D. (2010). Report of the Montara Commission of Inquiry. Canberra: Commonwealth of Australia. Available at: https://www.industry.gov.au/sites/default/files/2022-09/montara-commission-of-inquiry-report-june-2010.pdf (**Montara Report**).

[74] Montara Report at [3.289].

> *Q. So there is a widespread corporate cultural problem that involves reposing too much reliance upon those in the field and too little reliance upon a close consideration of information provided by them; do you agree?*
>
> *A. I would rather say too much reliance on personnel below each of those people, be it offshore or onshore. I don't think it is restricted to offshore.*
>
> *Q. Was the project manager a direct report to the CEO?*
>
> *A. Yes.*
>
> *Q. So, in all likelihood, we can go that one step further, too, can't we, sir, namely, that the CEO didn't properly inform himself of the nature and extent of the project manager's supervision of the affairs of the well construction department?*
>
> *A. It would appear so, yes.*
>
> *...*
>
> *Q. Will you accept, sir, that the nature of the evidence canvassed in the course of this Inquiry indicates deficiencies right up the line to and including the CEO of [PTTEPAA]?*
>
> *A. Yes, based on the line of questioning you have been following, yes.*[75]

This type of observation raises a question about how well suited our systems of workplace health and safety assurance, monitoring, and reporting are to inform the organisation and its leaders about the work health and safety risks associated with *"productive"* behaviours in the workplace.

A proactive, structured, and systematic approach to workplace health and safety

A duty holder must have a proactive approach to safety issues. The question is not whether the duty holder did envisage a particular danger, but rather whether they should have.[76]

---

[75] Montara Report, [3.291].

[76] *WorkCover Authority of New South Wales v Kellogg (Aust) Pty Ltd* [1999] NSWIRComm 453.

A duty holder must have a structured and systematic approach to risk management.[77]

In the Bros Bins case a worker was killed while doing repair work on a truck. In order to do the work, the worker had to raise a hydraulically operated jib at the back of the vehicle, with the jib locked in place by hooks that were operated pneumatically. While the worker was working on the rear of the vehicle the pneumatic hooks disengaged and the jib collapsed, killing the worker.

One of the allegations in the case was that the vehicle should have been fitted with a safety prop or other mechanism to support the jib while it was raised. There was evidence in the case to the following effect:

- there was no training about any procedures for people required to work under the raised section of the jib;
- people had not been informed that the jib could fall if the hooks were disengaged;
- people were not warned not to touch or otherwise interfere with any controls of the vehicle while the jib was raised; and
- the workers (in this case auto electricians) were all experienced workers but had been given no specific instructions about how to carry out their work.[78]

In looking at the obligations of the employer the court observed that employers must be vigilant an exercise foresight in all aspects of the work environment – *"It is not enough to comply with these obligations on an ad hoc basis looking at particular matters from time to time."*[79].

The court observed:

> *Whilst common sense might have dictated that a prop either be installed on the vehicle or utilised..., there was certainly no evidence of any structured approach to the provision of a prop at the [premises]. At best, there were materials which were lying around and which were used on an "as needed" basis in order to prop up equipment. ... there was no evidence of any systematic instruction or training [given to any employees] whether orally, in writing or a combination of both. neither was there any evidence of any supervision of any ad hoc understanding or arrangement*

---

[77] *Workcover Authority of NSW v Atco Controls Pty Ltd* (1998) 82 IR 80, 85; *Inspector Ching v Bros Bins Systems Pty Ltd* [2004] NSWIRComm 197, [32] (**Bros Bins**).

[78] Bros Bins, [29] – [30].

[79] Bros Bins, [31].

> *directed to minimising risks to health and safety at the workplace.*[80]
>
> ...
>
> *A casual act of negligence will only be relevant in circumstances where an employer has put in place a structured and organised system to identify and deal with the risks to health and safety including the instruction, training and supervision of employees and that the only reason for the particular risk to safety was a casual act of negligence on the part of an employee who had otherwise been properly instructed, trained and supervised which could not reasonably have been anticipated by the employer. This is not the case here.*[81]

Due diligence

Due diligence – at least in the Australian work health and safety context – is seen as a product of work health and safety legislation and the provisions of section 27 of the Model WHS Act which create positive obligations for officers of organisations to exercise due diligence in relation to the safety performance of the organisation.

I will discuss this *"individual"* concept of due diligence later, but it is also important to recognise that due diligence has *always* formed a critical element of discharging an organisation's obligations to do everything reasonably practicable:

> *Where an employer is found to have laid down a safe and proper practice and there is no evidence that the employer failed to use due diligence to see that the practice was observed, then a casual failure by inferior employees, even if of supervisory rank, to observe the practice on a particular occasion will not render the employer criminally liable for a failure to ensure safety.*[82]*:*

This organisational notion of due diligence is best understood in an Australian legal context as:

- having *"proper"* systems in place to ensure compliance with the relevant legislation; and

---

[80] Bros Bins, [33].

[81] Bros Bins, [33].

[82] *Collins v State Rail Authority of New South Wales* (1986) 5 NSWLR 209, 215 (**Collins**). See also Wollongong Glass, [32].

- adequate *"supervision"* to ensure the system is in place and effective.[83]

The notion of a *"proper system"* in the context of reasonably practicable means a system that ensures compliance with the work health and safety legislation.

When I run workshops, I often ask participants to explain what they think is required to demonstrate a proper system, and most of the initial examples describe elements of a system, not the characteristics of a system that make it "*proper*" in a reasonably practicable sense.

Training, for example, is an element of a workplace health and safety management system, but the fact that an organisation provides training is not evidence that the system is a proper system to achieve compliance. The same is true for the multitude of other elements that make up workplace health and safety management systems, such as:

- procedures;
- standards;
- frontline risk assessment tools like Take 5, JHA and safe work method statements;
- audits;
- inspections;
- management conversation; or
- investigations.

These are elements of your system but from a legal risk management perspective they are not evidence that you have a proper system. And at one level this should give comfort to people when deciding how to do safety because how you do safety does not really matter – there is no right way to do safety. What is important is that what you do "*works*".

But to return to the question of proper systems. In a legal risk management context, a proper system is one that aligns to the legal requirements.

A working at heights procedure is an element of a system to manage the risk of working at heights. But your system of working at heights is not a proper system if your working at heights procedure does not align with the requirements of relevant regulations, codes of practice or other standards, or guidance material issued by the regulator.

Of course, not every workplace hazard is captured by regulations or guidance material. In those circumstances, what does an organisation

---

[83] See for example *Universal Telecasters (Qld) Ltd v Gutherie* (1978) 18 ALR 531; *SafeWork NSW v Neville George Hetherington* [2019] NSWDC 11 (**Hetherington**).

point to, to demonstrate a proper system? Organisations can demonstrate they have proper systems in the absence of external guidance through their own, internal risk procedures – risk assessments, hazard and operability studies, working groups, references to industry practice and so on.

When the courts talk about supervision in the context of due diligence, they do not just mean what supervisors do. Supervision here refers to *"organisational"* supervision as well – whether the organisation has adequate, overarching, systems of assurance to know whether the *"proper systems"* are in place and effective.

In the Collins decision the defendant (the State Rail Authority of New South Wales) operated a rail repair plant. Some work was required on the roof of the building, and the defendant engaged a subcontractor to perform some of the work.

Electricity was provided to a foundry forming part of the worksite through 600 volt and 450-volt mains, and for the roofing work to be carried out, personnel had to work in relatively close proximity to the mains.

While working, one of the workers was electrocuted and died when a ladder he was moving contacted a bear clamp on one of the terminals of a sub-main.

The defendant was charged in relation to failures:

- on the basis that they failed to turn off the electricity supply; and
- the fact that the clamps that the ladder touched were not insulated.

Ultimately, the court found that the defendant had established proper systems to manage the risks associated with the electrical supply to the foundry, and there was no evidence that the defendant did not use due diligence in relation to those systems:

> *There was evidence that no inspections of the Crosby clamps were carried out but there was no evidence and no finding of fact to the effect that ordinary and proper practice required periodical inspection of the ends of the mains to confirm the existence of insulation on the Crosby clamps.*
>
> *It is apparent from the findings of fact that have been quoted that it was the practice in this establishment to bind the Crosby clamps with insulating tape. There was therefore no defective practice proved. How these particular clamps came to be bare of tape was not established in the evidence and there is every indication*

> *that this was due, as was the failure to isolate the foundry,*
> *to failure by one or more employees of the Authority in the*
> *fulfilment of the duties imposed upon them in respect of the*
> *ordinary practice of the electrical installations at the*
> *foundry.*[84]

Of course, we have already seen cases where organisations have, on the face of it, established proper systems to manage the workplace health and safety risks in their business but those systems were not implemented or effective. It is worth noting that this is not a new phenomenon.

In a 1948 decision[85] the court said:

> *A system of work is not devised by telling a man to read the*
> *regulations and not to break them. In the present case, in*
> *my view, no responsible person on behalf of the defendants*
> *had devised any system for doing this particular work. But*
> *even if it could be said that they had done so, by a long*
> *usage that paper system had, in practice, been utterly*
> *disregarded.*[86]

DUE DILIGENCE

Due diligence is not a new term, and indeed it is not a new concept in workplace health and safety. While a positive duty of due diligence was introduced into the Model WHS Act, due diligence was a defence available to individuals prosecuted under health and safety legislation in several Australian jurisdictions before the introduction of the Model WHS Act. Moreover, the basis underpinning principles of due diligence have always been relevant to individual liability – particularly management liability – under health and safety legislation, not just in Australia but in many other jurisdictions.

As we saw in the discussion about reasonably practicable, due diligence is an organisational obligation and an element of demonstrating that the organisation has done everything reasonably practicable.

Due diligence is also an individual responsibility, and expressly set out in Australian work health and safety legislation.

The due diligence obligations under Australian work health and safety legislation only apply to "*officers*" of the organisation – effectively directors, the company secretary, and the most senior managers of the organisation. A person can also be found to be an officer of an

---

[84]   Collins, pp. 216 – 217

[85]   *Barcock v Brighton Corporation* [1949] 1 K.B. 339 (**Brighton Corporation**).

[86]   Brighton Corporation, p. 343.

organisation by virtue of their decision-making capacity. The definition of officer extends to include a person:

- who makes, or participates in making, decisions that affect the whole, or a substantial part, of the business of the corporation; or
- who has the capacity to affect significantly the corporation's financial standing; or
- in accordance with whose instructions or wishes the directors of the corporation are accustomed to act (excluding advice given by the person in the proper performance of functions attaching to the person's professional capacity or their business relationship with the directors or the corporation).[87]

The obligations of due diligence are set out in section 27 of the Model WHS Act as follows:

27   Duty of officers

(1)   *If a person conducting a business or undertaking has a duty or obligation under this Act, an officer of the person conducting the business or undertaking must exercise due diligence to ensure that the person conducting the business or undertaking complies with that duty or obligation.*

(2)   *Subject to subsection (3), the maximum penalty applicable under Division 5 of this Part for an offence relating to the duty of an officer under this section is the maximum penalty fixed for an officer of a person conducting a business or undertaking for that offence.*

(3)   *Despite anything to the contrary in section 33, if the duty or obligation of a person conducting a business or undertaking was imposed under a provision other than a provision of Division 2 or 3 of this Part or this Division, the maximum penalty under section 33 for an offence by an officer under section 33 in relation to the duty or obligation is the maximum penalty fixed under the provision creating the duty or obligation for an individual who fails to comply with the duty or obligation.*

(4)   *An officer of a person conducting a business or undertaking may be convicted or found guilty of an*

---

[87]   The Model WHS Act references relevant definitions from the *Corporations Act 2001* (Cth), s9A

offence under this Act relating to a duty under this section whether or not the person conducting the business or undertaking has been convicted or found guilty of an offence under this Act relating to the duty or obligation.

(5)   *In this section, due diligence includes taking reasonable steps:*

(a)   *to acquire and keep up-to-date knowledge of work health and safety matters; and*

(b)   *to gain an understanding of the nature of the operations of the business or undertaking of the person conducting the business or undertaking and generally of the hazards and risks associated with those operations; and*

(c)   *to ensure that the person conducting the business or undertaking has available for use, and uses, appropriate resources and processes to eliminate or minimise risks to health and safety from work carried out as part of the conduct of the business or undertaking; and*

(d)   *to ensure that the person conducting the business or undertaking has appropriate processes for receiving and considering information regarding incidents, hazards and risks and responding in a timely way to that information; and*

(e)   *to ensure that the person conducting the business or undertaking has, and implements, processes for complying with any duty or obligation of the person conducting the business or undertaking under this Act; and*

Examples

For the purposes of paragraph (e), the duties or obligations under this Act of a person conducting a business or undertaking may include:

- *reporting notifiable incidents;*

- *consulting with workers;*

- *ensuring compliance with notices issued under this Act;*

- *ensuring the provision of training and instruction to workers about work health and safety;*

> • *ensuring that health and safety representatives receive their entitlements to training.*
>
> *(f)* *to verify the provision and use of the resources and processes referred to in paragraphs (c) to (e).*

Like reasonably practicable, this definition is subject to interpretation by the courts.

The due diligence obligation of officers is often mistakenly described as an obligation to ensure the safety of workers, or to ensure a safe workplace. The obligation is neither.

An officer must exercise due diligence to ensure that the *organisation is meeting its obligations* under the work health and safety legislation, and while due diligence includes, it is not limited to, the matters set out in subparagraph 5(a) – (f) described above:

> *[56]* *The section 27 duty imposed on officers is not to take all reasonably practical measures to ensure compliance by the PCBU and an officer is not required to ensure the health and safety of workers.*
>
> *[57]* *An officer is required to adhere to a minimum standard of behaviour involving a system which ensures compliance by the PCBU with its duties and obligations under the Act and to provide adequate supervision to ensure that the system is properly carried out. The minimal standard of behaviour and the system is to take reasonable steps to include the objectives in section 27(5) ...*
>
> *[58]* *Section 27 does not require that the officer undertake the reasonably practicable measures on behalf of the PCBU.*
>
> *[61]* *All of the case law on due diligence and the matters in section 27(5) ... refer to or are relevant to the systems put in place by an officer to ensure compliance by a PCBU, including obtaining the necessary knowledge of the Act and operation to implement such a system. Notwithstanding that the matters referred to in section 27(5) is not exhaustive, I am satisfied that any other relevant matters must in some way relate to the system implemented and enforced by an officer to ensure compliance by the PCBU.[88]*

---

[88] Hetherington.

While the scope of section 27 of the Model WHS Act has not been fully determined,[89] there are several principles which we can be confident apply.

First, the section 27 duty requires officers to take proactive steps to ensure compliance by the company.[90]

Second, due diligence refers to a minimum standard of behaviour that involves a system to prevent contravention of the work health and safety legislation, and adequate *"supervision"* to ensure that the system is *"properly carried out"*.[91] In this respect, personal due diligence is intimately linked to organisational obligations to do everything reasonably practicable.

Third, the systems designed to ensure the organisation is complying with its obligations under the work health and safety legislation must be *"appropriate and not a paper system designed to pay lip service to the Act and [the system must be] properly enforced to achieve compliance with the Act."*[92]

Fourth, the system must ensure that workers have the skills to perform the work, and ensure they comply with the safety standards established under the system, by formal and informal review and auditing.[93]

Fifth, directors need to address safety matters at board meetings and must require managers to report on safety matters. Directors must monitor safety as an issue.[94]

Sixth, due diligence requires assurance that supervisors and managers are acting in compliance with written policies and procedures.[95]

Case Studies

We do need to be careful when looking at case studies considering due diligence because most of the case studies looking at due diligence or related concepts for individuals under health and safety legislation in Australia prior to the Model WHS Act dealt with legal frameworks that were different from the positive obligations under section 27.

---

[89] See for example Hetherington.

[90] Hetherington, [38].

[91] *Universal Telecasters (Qld) Ltd v Gutherie* (1978) 18 ALR 531; Hetherington, [40].

[92] *Inspector Kumar v Ritchie* [2006] NSWIRComm 323, [153]; Hetherington, [41].

[93] *WorkCover Authority v Daly Smith Corporation* [2004] NSWIRComm 349, 152; Hetherington, [42].

[94] *Inspector Aldred v Herbert* [2007] NSWIRComm 170, [25]; Hetherington, [43].

[95] *Inspector Hayes v Santos and Lorenzo* [2009] NSWIRComm 163, [188]; Hetherington, [44].

Moreover, almost universally *"due diligence"* or similar prosecutions against individuals have been against small business owners close to the day-to-day operations of the business, rather than *"executive"* officers sitting in corporate headquarters and removed from day-to-day operations.[96]

That said, however, there does seem to be a level of consistency amongst cases and inquiries looking at executive management responsibilities which highlight issues around criticality, assumption, and systemic failure.

The rationale in many due diligence observations by courts and tribunals, although not expressly stated as such, seems to be that when critical safety processes are not in place, or not sufficient, or not being followed – or are otherwise deficient, the duty holder ought to have been aware that the system was not working. The lack of awareness may be evidence of a failure of due diligence. Moreover, if failures in critical elements of workplace health and safety management are not being brought to the duty holder's attention, then this may also be a failure of due diligence because the duty holder is not testing, questioning, or challenging the systems to understand if it is providing the right information.

Much of the legal argument in the context of due diligence is about extent to which the duty holder *"ought to have known"*. As we will see in some of the case studies moving forward, the question of what a duty holder knew or ought to have known turns on questions relating to the individual duty holder's position, knowledge, expertise, and other *"individual"* factors.

An important concept in the notion of due diligence is the extent to which a duty holder has, or is entitled to, make assumptions.

In my view the extent to which workplace health and safety management is underpinned by assumption is a very important element for both individuals and organisations trying to understand the efficacy of safety management in the organisation. We will see when discussing workplace health and safety metrics, the assumptions that underpin workplace health and safety metrics make them extraordinarily unreliable (if not dangerous) as indicators of the state of workplace health and safety.

---

[96] See for Example Foster, N. (2005). Personal Liability of Company Officers for Corporate Occupational Health and Safety Breaches: Section 26 of the Occupational Health and Safety Act 2000 (NSW). Australian Journal of Labour Law, 107.

Major accident inquiries regularly point to assumptions by senior managers as indicating a failure of due diligence.

On 6 July 1988, 167 people died following a catastrophic fire at the offshore oil producing platform, Piper Alpha. The subsequent inquiry into the disaster[97], identify the failure of the Permit to Work system as a critical causal factor in the disaster.

In part, the failure of the Permit to Work system was due to misplaced assumption on the part of management:

> *The managers who had responsibility for the correct operation of the [Permit to Work] system were all aware that the safety personnel on the platform were expected to monitor the daily operation of the system. All of them assumed that because they received no reports of failings the system was working properly. However, none of them check the quality of that monitoring nor did they carry out more than the most cursory examination of permits when they had occasion to visit Piper.[98]*

Many of the observation in the Piper Alpha inquiry were echoed more than 20 years later in the Pike River Royal Commission. In their observation about governance by the Pike River Board, the Royal Commission noted:

> *The board did not verify that effective systems were in place and that risk management was effective. Nor did it properly hold management to account, but instead assumed that managers would draw the board's attention to any major operational problems. The board did not provide effective health and safety leadership and protect the workforce from harm. It was distracted by the financial and production pressures that confronted the company.[99]*

Clearly, there is a genuine question for organisations and their leaders about the extent to which their understanding of the efficacy of workplace health and safety management is demonstrable, as opposed to being based on assumptions.

---

[97]   Cullen, L. (1990). The Public Enquiry into the Piper Alpha Disaster. London: HMSO (**Piper Alpha**).

[98]   Piper Alpha, p. 231

[99]   Panckhurst, H., Bell, S., & Henry, D. (2012). Royal Commission on the Pike River Coal Mine Tragedy - Volume 2. Wellington: Pike River Royal Commission. Retrieved December 24, 2017, p.18. From http://pikeriver.royalcommission.govt.nz/vwluResources/Final-Report-Volume-Two/$file/ReportVol2-whole.pdf (**Pike River Royal Commission**).

What also seems very important from the various cases is the distinction between what might be called a *"one-off"* departure from otherwise effective workplace health and safety management systems on the one hand, and evidence of long-term, systemic failure on the other.

Again, while it is not expressly explained in this way, long-term systemic failure of workplace health and safety management systems creates an inference of a lack of due diligence – a failure to pay proper attention to workplace health and safety – along the following lines:

> *If anyone was paying a reasonable level of attention to the management of workplace health and safety, the systems could not have broken down to the extent that they have.*

This idea of systemic failure often emerges in cases and inquiries. Looking again at Piper Alpha, we get the following observation:

> *Earlier in this report I reached the conclusion that a failure in the [Permit to Work (PTW)] system had occurred on the evening of the disaster and that if this had not occurred Mr Vernon would not have attempted to restart condensate injection pump A and thus unwittingly caused a leap of condensate... The evidence which I considered in Chapter 11 showed that this failure was not an isolated mistake but that in a number of respects the PTW system was being operated routinely in a casual and unsafe manner. That evidence along with the evidence to which I have referred to earlier in this chapter shows, in my view, the operation of the PTW system was not being adequately monitored or audited. These were failures for which management were responsible. If there had been adequate monitoring and auditing it is likely that these deficiencies in the PTW system would have been corrected.[100]*

Fry v Keating

Fry v Keating[101] is a Western Australian Supreme Court decision that predates the Model WHS Act and the positive due diligence obligations. Under the Western Australian legislation at the time an officer could be convicted of an offence if the company was convicted of an offence, and it could be shown that the same offence occurred because of the officer's consent, connivance, or neglect. While not a positive duty in the same way that due diligence under the Model WHS Act is, elements of the offence from a practical perspective are very similar.

---

[100] **Piper Alpha**, p. 231.
[101] [2013] WASC 109 (**Fry**).

In the Fry case, a worker was killed during lifting operations when a load being lifted by a crane slipped and fell. There was a *"proper"* process for doing the work, a method of lifting which the Court described as Method 1, but over time the workers had developed their own way of doing the work, Method 2.

Both the company and its two directors were prosecuted in relation to the fatality.

The Fry case calls out both *"assumption"* on behalf of the directors of the organisation, as well as systemic failure.

In relation to various assumptions on the part of the directors, the court noted:

> *At the outset, I should indicate that, in my view, the magistrate's uncontested findings referred to earlier are sufficient to enable the inference to be drawn, beyond reasonable doubt, that the Company's offence was attributable to neglect on the part of the directors. As McKechnie J observed in his reasons at [29], in effect, the directors assumed that the safe method (Method 1) was in use, but there were no procedures in place to ensure that the safe method was always used.*[102]

and

> *... the directors believed or thought that the yard supervisor, Mr Davies, was enforcing the use of Method 1.*[103]

The use of Method 2 on the day the incident was not a one-off departure. The use of Method 2 represented a systemic failure. The extent to which Method 2 had been normalised was underscored by the finding:

> *Five employees, who were recent employees prior to the accident, believed, based in part on instructions from more senior doggers/riggers, that Method 2 was the method to be used in moving L68 Packs at the workplace*[104]

There is an important observation tucked away in the decision which again speaks to assumption, but is very relevant in the context of the extent to which organisations and their leaders need assurance that the people they are relying on to discharge critical safety functions have the capacity to do so:

---

102 Fry, [32].
103 Fry, [19].
104 Fry, [19].

> *... Mr Davies administrative duties did not permit him to keep full attention to the yard...* [105]

Mr Davies was the yard supervisor and the fact that he was diverted from his yard duties by his administrative duties was a relevant factor in the extent to which the directors could rely on his *"supervision"* to help discharge their obligations.

A great deal of what organisations do to *"evidence"* the efficacy of workplace health and safety management relies on the conduct of frontline management. Yet very rarely do we ever see organisations confirm that frontline management had the capacity, in terms of training, skills, resources and probably most importantly time, to competently *"create"* that evidence.

A final observation on the Fry decision is extent to which the directors' role in the organisation and their technical experience/skill was influential in determining their liability. Relevant findings of fact included:

- the directors of the Company, Mr Decesare and Mr Keating, were experienced in an industry involving the slinging of loads, and both were qualified doggers and riggers; [106]
- each of the directors, Mr Decesare and Mr Keating, was 'hands on' in terms of being based at the workplace and frequently in the yard; [107] and
- the directors had discussed with the Yard Supervisor, Mr Davies, the appropriate method for slinging L68 Packs and had decided to use Method 1. [108]

Unfortunately, the Fry decision reinforces the increased liability of small business owners and directors who are close to the day-to-day performance of work. But otherwise, the Fry decision does emphasise the importance of understanding assumptions in organisations about the management of workplace health and safety, and the importance of recognising long-term non-compliance – systemic failure – with the processes to manage workplace health and safety.

---

[105] Fry, [18].
[106] Fry, [17].
[107] Fry, [17].
[108] Fry, [18].

Morrison v Winton; Morrison v Atlas Group Pty Ltd[109]

The Winton decision is another Western Australian Supreme Court decision where a director was charged with offences under the Western Australian occupational health and safety legislation. These were the same provisions that applied in the Fry decision, however in this case the General Manager Winton was acquitted.

The prosecution arose out of a workplace fatality that occurred when a worker was trapped in a paddle mixer that was reenergised.

Prior to the accident a worker, Mr Graham was working in a paddle mixer. Mr Graham had isolated the power to the mixer by engaging the emergency stop button and placing his tag on it. The Magistrate accepted that it was common practice for relevant machinery to be isolated using the emergency stop button, although there was a clear instruction that the power should have been isolated either from the local isolator switch attached to the machinery or the main isolator which would have isolated the whole of the brick press, including the linear grab and the paddle mixer. However, it was not in dispute that the isolator switch attached to the paddle mixer (referred to as the *"local isolator switch"*) was not working at the time of the accident.

At the same time, another worker, Mr Lengkeek was tasked to fix a defective linear grab on a brick press. Fixing the defective linear grab required the power to be reconnected.

A supervisor went and spoke to Mr Graham to tell him that the power needed to be reconnected for the other task, and on the evidence in the case, Mr Graham agreed to this, and the supervisor disengaged the emergency stop button, although Mr Graham's personal tag remained on it.

The supervisor gave evidence that he saw Mr Graham come down the stairs from the paddle mixer and leave the brick press area, apparently to go to the workshop.

According to the judgement:

> *The evidence establishes that after Graham left the paddle mixer, he went to the workshop and then returned to the mezzanine floor and the paddle mixer, and whilst the emergency switch was deactivated (so that the paddle mixer was "live") with Graham's tag still attached to it, Lengkeek, in the course of his work in trying to identify the electrical fault in the linear grab, in some way shorted out the switch*

---

[109] *Morrison v Winton; Morrison v Atlas Group Pty Ltd* BC9606040 (Unreported Supreme Court of Western Australia) (**Winton**).

> *that activated the paddle mixer motor. The effect of shorting out the switch was that the paddle mixer motor started. At that time, Graham was in the paddle mixer and as a result of the motor being switched on he was killed.[110]*

The Magistrate further noted the unusual combination of events and the "*freak*" nature of the accident:

> *It is to be noted in passing that the accident caused Graham's death was, undoubtedly, a freak accident in that it involved a number of contemporaneous coincidences. Firstly, the accident happened because Graham was in the paddle mixer, having originally told Stipanicev that he did not need to go back into the mixer and that it was safe to turn the power back on. Secondly, Graham's safety tag was left on the emergency stop switch, even after the power had been turned back on so that there was at least the possibility that when Graham returned from the workshop he may have mistakenly thought that the power was switched off as his tag remained on the emergency stop button. Thirdly, in a manner which cannot be ascertained, the switch which activated the paddle mixer was somehow shorted out so that the paddle mixer commenced to operate whilst Graham was inside. It is fair to say that the shorting out of that switch was truly a "freak accident" because the officers from Worksafe, who inspected the plant following the accident, were unable to replicate the way in which the paddle mixer accidentally commenced to operate. In that respect, Peter John White ("White"), an electrical inspector with Worksafe, testified that he attended the plant in his capacity as an "A" Grade Electrical Licensee for the purpose of inspecting the electrical installation. At transcript p264, White testified: "We used screwdrivers, test equipment, and so forth, to try and simulate, and we couldn't get it to go. As far as we - - from talking to the people - the electrician - - we had the electrician come down with and showed us exactly what he did as well, and we still couldn't get it to operate."*

> *White agreed with a suggestion in cross examination that the accident was a freak accident and he also agreed that neither he nor a second electrician, Mr Mancini, could make the motor start up by shorting it out.[111]*

---

[110] Winton, p. 5.
[111] Winton, p. 5.

One of the findings in the case was that if the local isolator switch had of been operational, and Mr Graham had activated it before commencing work, the shorting of the switch on the main control panel would not have activated promoter of the paddle mixer – effectively preventing the accident.

Both the magistrate and prosecution accepted that Winton did not have any specific knowledge of the defects which led to the accident. The argument proceeded on the basis that Mr Winton's state of *"actual"* knowledge was not relevant. Rather, the relevant question about Winton's state of knowledge was whether he *"ought to have known"* about the deficiencies, and that was an argument accepted by the Magistrate:

> *Where, as here, a statute is dealing with occupational safety and health, and with the responsibilities on an employer to provide and maintain a working environment in which his employees are not exposed to hazards, it is not sufficient for an employer to say that he had no knowledge of the particular risk. If that were the intention of the statute, then it would be in the interest of errant employers to deliberately avoid ascertaining the hazardous nature of the working environment so as to defeat the purpose of the statute. That cannot be the intention of the legislation.*[112]

While the company, Atlas Group was convicted of breaches of work health and safety legislation at the time, Winton as the General Manager was acquitted. The Magistrate found:

- the plant was a complex plant which employed several employees with different degrees of expertise, including electricians who are experts in their particular fields of work;
- it was unrealistic to expect that Winton would be sufficiently knowledgeable to understand all the risks associated with each aspect of the plant, unless particular faults were brought to his attention; and
- he had engaged a competent, expert safety officer who reported to from time to time in relation to safety aspects of the plant and he acted on recommendations made by the safety officer.

In all the circumstances, the failures by the company which led to the accident were not something which Winton ought to have known about, and he was acquitted.

---

[112] Winton, p. 8.

The legal framework

One of the important elements of the Winton case is that it reinforces that senior management in organisations are entitled to rely on the expertise of workers and their safety advisors, but it must be demonstrable that they were competent. In the case of the safety officer, the Magistrate specifically noted that they were competent in their capacity. I think it is also important to note that Winton was able to provide evidence that he acted on the recommendations made by the safety officer, or, where he did not immediately act on those recommendations, he was able to provide evidence to explain those circumstances:

> *The other aspect of the defence case at trial was that each of the defendants had been responsible for the employment of a safety officer who was competent in that capacity and whose recommendations were usually accepted and acted upon by management. There was one exception, however, which involved a recommendation that there should have been an occupational health and safety workshop for managers and supervisors. The safety officer at the time, Mr Ronald McKenzie Meechin ("Meechin") recommended to the management that they should hold an occupational health and safety workshop for managers and supervisors. Meechin testified at trial that this recommendation was not implemented by Winton who told him to "put that on hold". The reason for that, as revealed in the cross-examination of Meechin was because of the logistical difficulties of getting the managers and supervisors together at the one time for a safety course that may have taken some hours. With that exception, Meechin seemed to accept that most of his recommendations were acted upon, although there was clearly some apathy towards attending the safety sessions, particularly on the part of employees who were asked to attend those sessions during their lunch hour.*

> *In relation to that aspect of the case, in my opinion, it is fair to conclude that whilst Winton told Meechin to put the plan for a managers' and supervisors' workshop "on hold", that was capable of meaning, and in the context of this case did in fact mean, that Winton was prepared to allow Meechin to hold the training session as soon as it was practicable to do so.[113]*

---

[113] Winton, pp. 7 – 8.

The importance of ensuring the *"safety competence"* of advisers and others who are providing safety critical work was illustrated in another decision, the Ritchie decision.

The Ritchie decision[114]

The Ritchie decision is one of those rare cases that did involve the prosecution of an executive officer of an organisation who was far removed from the day-to-day operations of the business.

The Ritchie decision involved the prosecution of a company and two officers following the death of a worker in an explosion. The company, Owens Container Services Australia Pty Ltd was in the business of repairing, cleaning, and storing shipping containers and tanks. The accident occurred at one of their operations, referred to as the *"Race facility"*.

An employee was using a spray gun to spray methyl ethyl ketone (**MEK**) into a tank.

MEK is a highly volatile and highly flammable substance and had been used as a cleaning agent at the site. After spraying the tank for about five minutes with MEK, the tank was left for between 20 to 30 minutes.

When the employee returned, he used a high-pressure water spray gun to continue cleaning the tank, causing an explosion in which the employee sustained severe injuries and died shortly thereafter.

The company and one of the directors pleaded guilty to charges under the New South Wales health and safety legislation in place at the time.[115] A second director, Mr Richie pleaded not guilty.

Section 26 of the then *Occupational Health and Safety Act 2000* effectively created a reverse onus of proof whereby if the company breached the legislation, then each director of the corporation was taken to have breached the same provision, unless they could demonstrate either they:

- were not able to influence the conduct of the corporation in relation to its contravention of the provision, or
- if they were in in such a position, used all due diligence to prevent the contravention by the corporation.

The Court accepted prosecution submissions that to maintain a defence under the second part of section 26 (i.e., the due diligence requirement) the defendant needed to demonstrate:

---

[114] Inspector Ken Kumar v David Aylmer Ritchie [2006] NSWIRComm 323 (**Ritchie**).
[115] *Occupational Health and Safety Act 2000* (NSW).

- a systematic approach designed to achieve compliance with the Act;
- that the system was both proper and appropriate to achieve compliance with the Act - not merely some paper scheme that paid lip service to the Act or merely exaggerated the reality of the system that was in place; and
- the system was properly enforced and policed to prevent contraventions of the Act.[116]

By way of background, the Owens group was made up of 30 companies operating internationally with more than 1600 staff. Mr Richie was a resident of New Zealand and the Chief Financial Officer of the company at the time of the accident. He lived and worked in New Zealand and was the director of more than 10 Owens companies. Mr Richie had no prior experience with the operation of cleaning containers or ISO tanks.

The court may several findings of fact in relation to the accident, importantly:

- there were several workplace health and safety management systems in place;
- there was no qualified or proper auditing of those systems;
- there was no appropriate training in workplace health and safety generally or in risk assessment specifically;
- reliance was placed on a system of assumptions;
- personnel administering the system had no means of effectively enforcing the system;
- there was no evidence to show how enforcement was achieved;
- the person who undertook audits was not qualified to audit the tank wash procedure and did not have any training in dangerous goods;
- nothing was done to ensure that people employed as occupational health and safety officers were trained; and
- there was nothing in the system that would bring the lack of training to Mr Richie's attention.[117]

The Court observed:

> *The defendant's evidence, ultimately, relied upon a series*
> *of assumptions and reports he received from managers as*
> *well as audits in order to ensure the safety of the Race*

---

[116] Ritchie, [153].
[117] Ritchie, [154] – [155].

workforce. He assumed that the managers were doing their job.[118]

Consistent with other authority, the court confirmed that exercising due diligence required two responsibilities to be discharged. First *"the laying down of a proper system to provide against contraventions of the Act"*, and second *"providing adequate supervision to ensure that the system is properly carried out"*.[119] This could not be achieved by:

> *merely hoping others would or could do what they were told, but should ensure that they have the skills to execute the job they were required to perform and then ensure compliance in accordance with the safety standards established. Compliance required a process of reviewing and auditing, both formal and informal, in order to ensure that the same standards established were in fact being adhered to and under ongoing review.*[120]

Mr Richie had argued that the approach proposed by the prosecution in the case required an unreal level of detail in terms of what he should have known. The court rejected that saying:

> *What the defendant should have done was to make sure there was in place a system, not merely a paper system, that dealt with matters such as safety training, audits and risk assessments. A proper system did not necessarily require the defendant to be personally involved in having a detailed knowledge of every aspect of the safety features at the Race facility, but it would have involved the implementation and enforcement of fundamental safety procedures. In this case, nothing was done over a long period of time to rectify long-standing serious shortcomings at the Race facility.*[121]

Ultimately, Mr Richie was convicted.

The reference in the Ritchie decision to *"fundamental safety procedures"*, speaks to another very important element of assurance - *criticality.*

There are many elements of workplace health and safety management, including workplace health and safety metrics, which target an extremely broad range of workplace health and safety information. Often workplace health and safety information is relatively trivial, and in some cases focusing on less *"fundamental"* aspects of

---

[118] Ritchie, [157].
[119] Ritchie, [151].
[120] Ritchie, [152].
[121] Ritchie, [160].

workplace health and safety can blind organisations to critical risk in the business.

This was a theme picked up by the Pike River Royal Commission:

> *The statistical information provided to the board on health and safety comprised mainly personal injury rates and time lost through accidents ... The information gave the board some insight but was not much help in assessing the risks of a catastrophic event faced by high hazard industries. ... The board appears to have received no information proving the effectiveness of crucial systems such as gas monitoring and ventilation.*[122]

This observation not only recognises limitations of injury rate data as a measure of safety performance, but it also emphasises the importance of testing the efficacy of crucial systems.

The Bata decision[123]

The Bata decision is a Canadian environmental case, which might seem an odd choice of case study for a book looking at workplace health and safety largely grounded in an Australian regulatory framework. However, the Bata decision was cited in the review that was part of establishing the Model WHS Act, noting:

> *A test for due diligence commonly referred to is that spelt out in [the Bata decision] which: requires that a defendant director must show in relation to [workplace health and safety] that:*
>
> 1. *They were familiar with their Occupational Health & Safety obligations and relevant codes of practice and industry standards;*
>
> 2. *They had a system in place to manage occupational health and safety risks and that they adequately supervised compliance with that system;*
>
> 3. *The system complied with industry standards and practices;*
>
> 4. *Company officers reported back to the board on the operation of the system and safety concerns were reported in a timely manner;*

---

122 Pike River, p. 53
123 *R v Bata Industries Ltd* (1992) 7 CELR 245 (**Bata**).

> 5. *They reacted personally and immediately upon becoming aware of the system failure.*[124]

The Bata decision was also referenced in the *"Due Diligence Index"*,[125] so evidently the Bata decision does have some influence from a policy and principle perspective.

The Bata decision is also a useful case in the broader context of understanding if our *"systems"* are implemented and effective.

The Bata decision related to offences arising from environmental damage associated with the operation of a shoe manufacturing business. The damage was caused by chemical waste leaking from drums and barrels stored on site.

From a due diligence perspective, the case is interesting because it involved the prosecution of the company and three different levels of management. The various managers were prosecuted for failing to take reasonable care to prevent the discharge, however, it was open to the managers to argue a due diligence defence. The due diligence defence as described in the case was that the defendants:

> *"exercised all reasonable care by establishing a proper system to prevent commission of the offence and by taking reasonable steps to ensure the effective operation of the system."*[126]

Having regard to the discussion of reasonably practicable and due diligence already in this book, it should be readily apparent why the Bata decision is relevant to the broader consideration of Proving Safety.

The three managers who were prosecuted were:

- Mr Thomas G Bata, a director, who was acquitted;
- Mr Douglas Marchant, the president of the board, who was convicted; and
- Mr Keith Weston, the on-site director who was also convicted.

The Court dealt with each of the managers in turn.

---

[124] *National Review into Model Occupational Health and Safety Laws*, Second Report to the Workplace Relations Ministers Council, January 2009, Commonwealth of Australia, pp 59 – 60 (**WHS Review**).

[125] The Bata decision was referenced in the context of *"vigilantly verifying the implementation of processes and resources deployed to address risks and ensure compliance"*.

[126] Bata, [41].

Mr Thomas G Bata

In relation to Mr Thomas G Bata, the court identified that he was the director with the least personal contact at the plant and his responsibilities were primarily directed at the global level of the organisation.

The court found that Mr Bata attended the site once or twice a year to review the operations and he was described as a walk around director while on-site, and plant managers could not orchestrate a visit for him. Specific evidence referred to by the court was:

> _"You never knew where Mr Bata was going to go, believe me. He had a habit of trying to out guess where you wanted him to go."[127]_

It was also established that when an engineering solution for the chemical storage problem was brought to Mr Bata's attention, he immediately addressed the issue with what the court described as _"appropriate resources ($20,000)"[128]_ to minimise the effect on the environment

The court found:

> _in short, [Mr Bata] was aware of his environmental responsibilities and he had written directions to that effect... He did personally review the operation when he was on-site and did not allow himself to be wilfully blind or orchestrated in his movements. He responded to matters when brought to his attention promptly and appropriately.[129]_

Douglas Marchant

The court described Mr Marchant responsibilities as greater than Mr Bata's but less than Mr Weston's.[130]

The evidence established that Mr Marchant went to the plant once a month and that the storage problems were brought to his personal attention which meant, relevantly, that he had personal knowledge of the issues for at least six months. At the time alleged in the charges and there was no evidence that he took any steps after having gained this knowledge to view the site and assess the problems and there was no

---

[127] Bata, [155].
[128] Bata, [156].
[129] Bata, [157].
[130] Bata, [160].

evidence that the system of storage was made safer, or that temporary safety steps were taken.[131]

Relevantly the evidence established that:

- $100,000 had been set aside for disposal of the waste in March 1988;

- quotes to dispose of the chemicals were requested in January 1989;

- quotes had been received by April 1989; however

- no action was taken until 11 August 1989 when relevant regulators were on-site.

The court observed:

> *In the circumstances it is my opinion that due diligence requires him to exercise a degree of supervision and control that "demonstrate that he was exhorting those whom he may be normally expected to influence or control to an accepted standard of behaviour."*

> *He had a responsibility not only to give instructions, but also to see to it that those instructions were carried out in order to minimise damage. The delay in cleanup showed a lack of due diligence.[132]*

Mr Keith Weston

Mr Weston had responsibilities as an *"on-site"* director, and the court noted that this made him *"much more vulnerable to prosecution"*.[133]

There was an interesting observation made by the court in relation to Mr Weston's obligations considering quotations received to deal with the waste products.

In July 1986, the company issued a Technical Advisory Circular (**TAC**) 298 with particular attention to environmental concerns, requesting the various companies to work in cooperation with local authorities to identify problems and carry out precautionary measures. The first recommendation in TAC 298 was an assessment of environmental exposure and reduction of potential risk.

When TAC 298 was issued the on-site environmental officer, Mr De bruyn, discussed the chemical waste drum storage problem with Mr Weston. Mr Weston instructed Mr De bruyn to get a quote for the cost of removing the waste and in late 1986 or early 1987 Mr De bruyn advised

---

[131] Bata, [161] – [162].
[132] Bata, [164] – [165].
[133] Bata, [169].

Mr Weston that the quote was $56,000. The evidence was that Mr Weston's response to the quote was:

> *"I was extremely surprised. I felt it was a large sum of money. It is an area of business that I know absolutely nothing about, so I had no way of knowing if it was high or considerably too high. So I instructed Mr De bruyn to get me an alternative quote."*[134]

Having made this observation, the court referred to the following passage of cross examination:

> Q. *Did you ever speak to anyone personally at Tricel?*
>
> A. *No.*
>
> Q. *And you felt the quote was too high?*
>
> A. *I felt that I needed an alternative, I did not have sufficient information to accept that quote per se, I needed an alternative quote to assess its value.*
>
> Q. *... Surely you must have looked at some writings, some memos or letters from Tricel, did not you?*
>
> A. *No, I was informed by Mr De bruyn that was the quotation that had been given.*
>
> Q. *And you felt that was too high?*
>
> A. *I felt it would be irresponsible to spend money without getting an alternative quote.*
>
> Q. *Between late 1986 in late 1987... did you ever think of phoning up the Ministry of Environment and asking them what should be done with the waste?*
>
> A. *Personally, I did not, no.*
>
> Q. *Did you ever contact anyone who might have knowledge about environmental matters to give you some advice? By that, I mean a consultant?*
>
> A. *No... I passed the, the problem was in the hands of the safety and environmental officer, and he was dealing with it.*
>
> Q. *And the safety and environmental officer was Mr De bruyn?*
>
> A. *Yes.*
>
> Q. *And was not it your understanding he certainly did not have any environmental training, did he?*
>
> A. *Specific training for environmental control – no.*[135]

---

[134] Bata, [67].
[135] Bata, [68].

The court went on to note that in late 1987, an alternative quote for $28,000 was obtained and Mr De bruyn was instructed to go ahead and accept the quotation and remove the waste. However, in early autumn of 1988, Mr Weston was advised of the contractor could not honour their agreement to clear the waste.

This, and presumably other evidence, lead the court to make some interesting observations in relation to Mr Weston which are worth setting out in full:

> *In addition to the evidence previously related in respect to the due diligence of [the company], it is my opinion, red flags should have been raised in his environmental consciousness when the first quote of $58,000 was obtained. Instead of simply dismissing it out of hand, he should have enquired why it was so high and investigated the problem. I find that he had no qualms about accepting the second quote of $28,000, and he had no further information other than it was cheaper. This was not an informed business judgement, and he cannot rely upon the business judgement rule, which at its core recognises that a business corporation is profit oriented and that an honest error of judgement should not impose liability provided the requisite standard of care is met.*

> *I find confirmation in this opinion by the fact that when he was transferred in November, he allocated $100,000 to waste disposal, again without any further knowledge. One cannot help but wonder if his diminished incentive package was a motivating factor in the allotment of $100,000 at this time. This expense would only affect him personally to the amount of $500 because the company was now in a profit position and his salary incentive based on reducing losses was minimal.*

> *It is my finding that Keith Weston cannot shelter behind the advice he received from Mr De bruyn. As Bata was "cut to the bone" by Mr Weston, the additional responsibilities fell upon Mr De bruyn and grossly overloaded him. The problem was aggravated by the interference from the evidence that Mr De bruyn was not given the authority to expend the $58,000 or the $28,000 on his own. He required the approval of Mr Weston. In my opinion, the failings of Mr De bruyn fall on the shoulders of Mr Weston,...*

> *As the "on-site" director, Mr Weston had a responsibility in this type of industry to personally inspect on a regular basis, i.e., "walkabout." To simply look at the site "not too*

> *closely" 20 times over his four-year tenure does not meet the mark. He had an obligation if he decided to delegate responsibility, to ensure that the delegate received the training necessary for the job, and to receive detailed reports from that delegate."[136]*

FINAL THOUGHTS

I think a particularly interesting juxtaposition in the Winton case, the Ritchie case, and the Bata case, is the reliance management placed on their relevant advisors.

In the Winton case, the court simply noted that the *"safety officer was competent in that capacity."*[137] There does not appear to be any dispute that the defendant, Mr Winton, could rely on the safety officer's advice.

In contrast, in the Ritchie decision, the court noted:

> *"This alleged system as overseen by the defendant permitted a person to be appointed to a position of occupational health and safety officer who had no relevant experience, training or qualifications for that position..."[138]*

And finally, in Bata, we have the observation:

> *"It is my finding that Keith Weston cannot shelter behind the advice he received from Mr De bruyn. As Barter was "cut to the bone" by Mr Weston, the additional responsibilities fell on Mr De bruyn and grossly overloaded him... In my opinion, the failings of Mr De bruyn fell on the shoulders of Mr Weston..."[139]*

This issue of *"reliance"* was dealt with again by the New South Wales District Court, just as this book was about to be published.

On 8 March 2024, the NSW District Court handed down a decision which is one of the first cases to meaningfully consider the conduct of an officer charged with a due diligence offence under work health and safety legislation.[140]

In November 2020, a worker was assisting a forklift operator load a truck and was hit by the moving forklift suffering serious injuries.

---

[136] Bata, [170] – [171].
[137] Winton, p. 18.
[138] Ritchie, [157].
[139] Bata, [172].
[140] *SafeWork NSW v Miller Logistics Pty Ltd; SafeWork NSW v Mitchell Doble* [2024] NSWDC 58 (**Doble**).

The company, Miller Logistics, was described by the court as a medium sized company which operated over 8 sites. The company was in voluntary liquidation by the time of the hearing, and there was no appearance on behalf of the company, which was convicted.

Mr Doble was the sole director of the company.

The court found that there was a clear risk of workers being struck by a forklift when they were loading vehicles in the workplace, and that the company recognised this risk, but the only precaution it took was to adopt a "*3m rule*".

The court found that the 3m rule was totally inadequate, and there was no clarity about what it meant. As described by the court it was a phrase that was used "*from time to time*" but there was no document to clarify what the rule was. The court said at best,

> *... it seems to have been an exhortation to workers on foot to stay at least 3m away from a forklift. That unsophisticated 'rule' amounted to little more than saying the workers on foot 'look out for yourself'. This this is always an inadequate precaution to take, when there are reasonably practicable measures of ensuring safety.*[141]

The charge against the company particularised that it was reasonably practicable for the company to:

- provide designated loading and unloading zones;
- provide designated and clearly marked forklift lanes;
- provide designated and clearly marked pedestrian exclusion zones; and
- install physical barriers in the loading and unloading areas to separate pedestrians and power mobile plant.

All these measures were taken after the incident and the court said that the company should have taken "*each and every one*" of those steps before the incident.

The summons against Mr Doble alleged that he failed to exercise due diligence in two respects. First, he failed to ensure the company had available for use, and used, appropriate resources and processes to eliminate or minimise risk. Part of the summons set out that Mr Doble should have carried out his duty of due diligence by "*requiring, instructing or directing*" the company to take the reasonably practicable steps which the company should have taken to ensure safety.

---

[141] Dobel, [239].

Second it was alleged that Mr Doble failed to verify that one or more of the resources or processes were actually provided, implemented, and used by workers when undertaking work for or on behalf of the company.

However, the court said that the allegations against Mr Doble did not set out what he should have done to exercise due diligence:

> *Having said that, the Doble Summons does not actually plead what Mr Doble should have done to discharge his duty of due diligence. To put it in terms of the legislation, the Doble Summons does not particularise the ways in which Mr Doble failed to exercise due diligence, beyond essentially saying that he should have done something to ensure that [the company] complied with its duty. What that something was is not elucidated...*[142]

The court found that there were specific steps taken by Mr Doble that show he exercised due diligence. These included:

- weekly management meetings were work health and safety was an agenda item;
- if a work health and safety matter needed to be dealt with it was attended to quickly;
- Mr Doble was in contact with the staff member responsible for work health and safety, Mr Hayter, and kept himself informed about what was being done by him;
- new safety measures were raised and discussed at management meetings;
- if a safety matter was raised and a task set to address it there was discussion at the next meeting ensure it had been completed and the steps were minuted;
- Mr Doble attended different work sites from time to time and if he observed a problem, he asked for it to be fixed;
- Mr Doble took an active interest in ensuring work health and safety was complied with;
- if there was an urgent matter Mr Doble would get involved; and
- there was evidence that there was no budgetary constraint to fixing work health and safety matters.

The court said that a managing director in the position of Mr Doble could not know everything that was going on in the business at any given moment. To run a corporation there must be a level of delegation.

---

[142] Doble, [261].

In the context of delegation, the court noted that Mr Doble was entitled to rely on Mr Hayter, who was specifically employed to deal with WHS:

> *The evidence in the case shows that Mr Hayter was specifically employed to deal with work health and safety. This required Mr Hayter to not only update policies and procedures, but to deal with any issues which arose from time to time. There was no suggestion in the evidence that Mr Hayter was anything other than conscientious. There was no suggestion in the evidence that Mr Doble had any reason not to place confidence in Mr Hayter carrying out his work health and safety duties. The engagement of Mr Hayter was the primary process or resource which Mr Doble used to ensure that the PCBU carry out its duty under the WHS Act.[143]*

Ultimately the court said that:

- Mr Doble was not a *"hands-off"* director in relation to work health and safety and he took an active interest in ensuring that work health and safety and compliance were attended to;
- there was a system to identify and manage safety risks and to ensure that these were addressed; and
- there were resources and processes and verification steps to ensure that the system was followed.

The court held that these steps were sufficient to meet Mr Doble's due diligence obligations.

When we come to look at the issues of metrics in workplace health and safety management and the broader question of a framework for Proving Safety, a key issue will be the level of assumption that underpins workplace health and safety management.

Importantly, and in my experience, there is nothing in the management systems designed to provide assurance about the efficacy of workplace health and safety management that works, or perhaps more correctly, is even designed, to recognise, make overt and test the assumptions that underpin workplace health and safety management.

Consider your own circumstances for a moment.

What evidence do you have that the people in your organisation who are responsible for developing, implementing, and overseeing workplace health and safety management have the confidence, capacity, and resources to do it effectively?

---

[143] Doble, [265].

More contemporaneously, in Australia at the time of writing this book, psychosocial risk is at the forefront of workplace health and safety regulation. In that specific context, what evidence do you have that your workplace health and safety personnel, who may have traditionally advised you on "*normal*" physical work health and safety risks, have the competence, capacity, and resources (or access to expert advice) to manage workplace psychosocial risks?

As I said in the opening to this Part of the book, in some senses the legal framework underpinning workplace health and safety obligations is straightforward and linear. However, in other respects, the practical application of compliance measures against that framework can be very difficult.

What the history of case law and public inquiries does teach us is that criticality, assumptions, and systemic failure are all important ideas that need to be understood and interrogated as part of any attempt by an organisation to understand if the systems in place to manage workplace health and safety are fit for purpose and effective.

The idea of criticality in understanding the efficacy of workplace health and safety management creates a broad range of questions and requires an organisation to make some conscious risk-based decisions.

At one level in the context of *"high risk"* activities, criticality is reasonably straightforward in relation to those activities. For example, in Pike River the statement by the Royal Commission that the organisation needed to prove the effectiveness of crucial systems such as gas monitoring and ventilation makes perfect sense. Gas monitoring and ventilation in the context of underground coal mining are clearly critical.

Similarly, when the Piper Alpha inquiry calls out the importance of the permit to work system is not difficult to understand the criticality of that process both in the specific context of the disaster, and more generally in the control of significant risks on offshore platforms. I do not think the identification of the permit work system as a critical process in the Piper Alpha inquiry was something done with the benefit of hindsight – it was both knowable and known to the industry before the disaster. The same holds true for gas monitoring and ventilation in the context of underground coal mining as called out by the Pike River Royal Commission.

Criticality in other contexts, however, may not be so straightforward. If we look to the *"fundamental"* safety procedures identified in the Ritchie decision, they include safety training, audits, and risk assessments. *"Proving effectiveness"* of those potentially crucial systems is likely to be more difficult. But what will become apparent when we look at a proposed framework for proving safety, is that the organisation and its leaders need to receive information and ask questions that both demonstrate and challenge the efficacy of critical *"system level"* processes. These system level processes are critical because they underpin the safety of all activities, and include things such as:

- training;
- supervision;
- audits;[144]
- risk assessment;
- management of change; and
- contractor safety management.

In other words, criticality is not confined to specific high-risk activities, hazards, or procedures. Criticality needs to account for important overarching processes designed to underpin the entire process of workplace health and safety management. How is it that an organisation gets assurance that its overall *"system"* of workplace health and safety training is fit for purpose, implemented, and works – how do we *"prove the effectiveness"* of workplace health and safety training? I will argue in my discussion on metrics that it is not by counting the percentage of training completed against targets.

Indeed, and as I hope to show, creating a metric based on counting the percentage of training completed against targets is a very good example of how assumptions which underpin so much of what we do in workplace health and safety management have the potential to create illusions of safety and undermine the efficacy of workplace health and safety management.

So much of what is done in the name of workplace health and safety management necessarily must carry a level of assumption with it – it is not feasible in any organisation to operate in a state of permanent assurance.

---

[144] I have not included specific commentary about audits in this book, but it is evident that audits as a mechanic to *"prove safety"* are equally susceptible to assumptions and corruption as any other workplace health and safety metric discussed. For some insightful discussion on the issues with audits, see: Hutchinson, B., Dekker, S., & Rae, A. (2024). Audit masquerade: how audits provide comfort rather than treatment for serious safety problems. Safety science, 169, 106348; Hutchinson, B., Dekker, S., & Rae, A. (2024). How audits fail according to accident investigations: A counterfactual logic analysis. Process Safety Progress; Do audits improve the safety of work? See also, The Safety of Work Podcast, Ep 116. Do audits improve the safety of work? | The Safety of Work

The legal framework

The challenge for an organisation, in my view, is to understand where the assumptions reside in their workplace health and safety management systems and to determine how much time, effort and energy the organisation wants to devote to testing those assumptions.

For example, a Queensland coroner's inquiry[145] which considered a daily service check on a vehicle, found:

> *Operating crew members stated to the Queensland Transport investigator that a complete adherence to the checklist was time-consuming. Consequently, the usual practice was for a random crew member to conduct cursory checks only on the key items relating to lubrication, calling and work had mechanisms. The entire checklist would then usually be marked to indicate compliance.*
>
> *I agree with the Queensland Transport investigator who was of the view that this "tick and flick" practice, over time, eroded the assurance that was intended to be provided by the checklist. It permitted a technically unserviceable Track Machine to operate in work mode within a work site. ... It is my view that this failure is likely to have contributed to the deaths of Mr Adams and Mr Watkins.*

If daily service checks on equipment are an important part of an organisation's work health and safety management systems, how much time and effort is the organisation prepared to expend to understand if they are being done properly or are effective to manage the risks associated with the operation of that equipment?

Perhaps more controversially, is the idea that the people performing the work are the people best placed in the organisation to develop the processes to manage the health and safety risks associated with that work? Surely that cannot be a universal truism that is always correct. From a legal risk management perspective, however individual workgroups might feel about the best way to safely perform their work, surely there ought to be account taken of any strict legal requirements. But regardless, to what extent are we prepared to test and challenge the assumption that people performing the work are the people best placed in the organisation to develop processes to manage the health and safety risks? Again, I think it would be difficult to conceive of the process where workgroups were left entirely to their own devices.

---

[145] Non-inquest findings into the deaths of Jamie Christopher ADAMS and Gary Robert WATKINS, 2018, p. 8.

I recall several years ago being involved in the investigation of an horrific workplace accident, and while presenting my findings to the board I started making observations about the problems with the complex and bureaucratic management systems that applied to the task being performed. I made comments to the effect that the workers, and the supervisor who was killed in particular, probably needed more discretion in how they manage the work. The then chief executive officer as part of that discussion identified, quite correctly in my view, that part of the problem was that the supervisor was exercising their discretion in a way that likely caused his own death.

If workers design their own systems of work to manage the workplace health and safety risks associated with that work, that "*philosophy*" in no way diminishes an organisation's obligations to understand if the general system works (i.e., does the general philosophy that workers can design their systems of work "*work*"), and the specific application of that system (i.e., is each individual system of work operating effectively to manage the specific risks of that work).

Any process of workplace health and safety management, whether New View or Traditional, carries with it certain assumptions. If those assumptions are not surfaced – if they are not overtly acknowledged and tested from time to time – it can lead to an ill-founded illusion about the state of workplace health and safety management in organisations and sow the seeds for future catastrophe.

Ongoing, untested assumptions about the state of workplace health and safety in an organisation, the application of workplace health and safety processes, and the underpinning basis for workplace health and safety measures can create the foundation for ongoing, long-term, systemic non-compliance with basic workplace health and safety management requirements in an organisation. A critical focus for organisations and their leaders must be to assess any potential weakness in workplace health and safety management not just on the merits of the specific circumstances, but as a warning or potential indicator of systemic failure.

While many organisations are responsive to weaknesses in their workplace health and safety management processes and identify and address concerns through processes such as hazard reporting, audits and reviews, and incident investigations, very often those processes and responses do not progress beyond the circumstances of the individual event. For example, an organisation may investigate an incident, it may develop learnings, may identify root causes, it may develop corrective actions – but typically all those things are in the context of the specific incident. If the response extends beyond the specific incident, often it only extends insofar as the same "*type*" of activity is being done in the organisation or on other sites controlled by the organisation. We want to address like for like issues.

And we must address like for like issues. We would be liable and in breach of our obligations if we did not address like for like issues.

But we often fail to use events as a trigger to search for potential warning signs of systemic failure.

If a causal finding in an incident investigation is that a procedure was not fit for purpose, then obviously that specific procedure must be reviewed and addressed. However, the broader systemic questions include:

- Why was the procedure not fit for purpose?
- Is there something systemic in the way that we develop procedures that has led to this outcome?
- Is it just this procedure that is not fit for purpose, or is that a problem more broadly in the organisation?

From any view of what might constitute reasonably practicable or due diligence, simply addressing a single poor procedure is not sufficient. We need to understand why a poorly developed procedure was able to be incorporated into our work practices in the first place, and the extent to which poor procedures may exist across our operations.

Similarly, any finding in an incident investigation that a causal factor was "*inadequate*" supervision cannot just be dealt with by addressing supervision in the context of that incident or supervisor. The question must be asked as to what does inadequate supervision, in any specific circumstance, tell us about our systems of supervision more broadly?

Any consideration of legal risk management from a workplace health and safety perspective requires an understanding of, and deep consideration with respect to, the following questions:

- Do we know whether our systems for managing health and safety risks in a workplace are proper systems that comply with the requirements of the regulatory framework?
- Do we know whether our systems for managing health and safety risks in our workplace are implemented and effective?

One of the challenges I would like to present in this book, having regard to the two questions posed above, and the principles of reasonably practicable and due diligence that I have examined, is whether an organisation's current systems of workplace health and safety reporting, and current workplace health and safety metrics, give any insight at all into any of these questions and principles.

The legal framework

PART 5
SAFETY AS A WICKED PROBLEM

"The usual duty of the "intellectual" is to argue for complexity and to insist that phenomena in the world of ideas should not be sloganized or reduced to easily repeated formulae."[146]

---

[146] Christopher Hitchens

Safety as a wicked problem

In their seminal paper, *Dilemmas in a General Theory of Planning*[147], the authors opined that the search for a scientific basis for dealing with problems of social policy was bound to fail because of the nature of those problems. They are *"wicked"* problems.

Wicked problems are broadly characterised by the following:

- they cannot be definitively described;
- they cannot be objectively described in terms of true or false; and
- there are no *"best"* solutions, indeed there may be no solutions at all in terms of definitive and objective answers.

Social policy questions, like workplace safety, are difficult to formulate by reference to goals – what should our systems directed to workplace safety *do*?

The complexity of goal formation is partly illustrated is the previous discussions about what is safe or safety. The fact the Model WHS Act says:

> The **<u>main object of this Act</u>** is to provide for a balanced and nationally consistent framework to secure the health and safety of workers and workplaces ...[148] (my emphasis added),

speaks to the complexity of the objectives of safety policy.

Providing for a *"balanced and nationally consistent framework"* is an attempt to put a boundary around the problem workplace safety – it is not a solution to the problem.

Consistent with the difficulty of goal formation (and perhaps in part a cause of it) is problem definition. As the authors of Wicked Problems note:

> By now we are all beginning to realise that one of the most intractable problems is that of defining problems (of knowing what distinguishes an observed condition from a desired condition) and of locating problems (finding where in the complex causal networks the trouble really lies). In turn, and equally intractable, is the problem of identifying the actions that might effectively narrow the gap between what-is and what-ought-to-be. As we seek to improve the effectiveness of actions in pursuit of valued outcomes, as system boundaries get stretched, and as we become more

---

147 Rittel, H.W.J. and Webber, M.M. (1973) *Dilemmas in a General Theory of Planning.* Policy Sciences, 4, 155-169 (**Wicked Problems**).

148 https://www.safeworkaustralia.gov.au/sites/default/files/2022-06/model_whs_bill_-_14_april_2022.pdf.

> *sophisticated about the complex workings of open societal
> systems, it becomes ever more difficult to make the planning
> idea operational.[149]*

And who in safety has not struggled with how to operationalise the views of Safety Differently?

The authors identify that planning and governance problems are inherently wicked problems and describe 10 characteristics which distinguish wicked problems from *"tame"* problems.

I note before we continue that tame problems are not necessarily simple, but tame problems have clear objectives, and we can determine when the problem is solved. Putting a person on the moon was not easy or simple, but the mission was clear, the technical problems solvable, and we could say when the objective has been achieved:

> *The problems that scientists and engineers have usually
> focused on a mostly "tame" or "benign" ones. As an
> example, consider a problem of mathematics, such as
> solving an equation; or the task of an organic chemist in
> analysing the structure of some unknown compound; or
> that of the chess player attempting to accomplish
> checkmate in five moves. For each the mission is clear. It is
> clear, in turn, whether or not the problems have been
> solved.*
>
> *Wicked problems, in contrast, have neither of these
> clarifying traits; and they include nearly all public policy
> issues – whether the question concerns the location of the
> freeway, the adjustment of the tax rate, the modification of
> school curricula, or the confrontation of crime.[150]*

The same I would argue is true for health and safety in the workplace.

Of course, within the broad church of workplace health and safety there are specific technical elements that are clearly engineering, scientific, or *"tame"* problems.

For example, the question of how to erect a scaffold so it is safe and secure is a technical problem best answered by technical experts. And the question of whether a scaffold has been erected safely is also a technical question, which can be answered and addressed by technical experts checking or *"auditing"* the scaffold.

The workplace health and safety *"system"* problem is not tame.

---

[149] Wicked Problems, p. 159
[150] Wicked Problems, p. 160.

The workplace health and safety systems surrounding an apparent, straightforward technical task like erecting scaffold are not so straightforward, an observation which is reinforced by continual workplace accidents involving scaffolding.

When we analyse workplace safety in the context of the authors' characterisation of wicked problems, I think it is self-evident that safety is a wicked problem, and our attempts to prove that workplaces are *"safe"* is unrealistic and pointless. At best the measures we think demonstrate our workplaces are safe provide prompts for further questions and inquiry – and if all this book does is shift that mindset, then that is a small success.

But to the point, what are the characteristics of a wicked problem, and is workplace health and safety one?

There is no definitive formulation of a wicked problem

Tame problems are knowable, and it is possible (albeit with the right technical expertise) to formulate a definitive list of the information needed to understand and solve the problem. This does not appear to be true for workplace health and safety.

What is the nature of the workplace health and safety problem we are trying to solve? Does the answer look different if people really are the solution to the problem – if these two binary propositions really exist.

And what happens if, in solving one *"view"* of safety, we create or exacerbate another safety problem?

Most health and safety legislation in Australia expressly includes psychological health within its remit.[151] Even in cases where psychological health was not expressly confirmed in Australian legislation, regulators accepted that psychological health was part of their remit. For example, in 2015 the Western Australian Department of Mines and Petroleum acknowledged that they regard *"health"* as including *"psychological"* health, even though the State's mining legislation at the time did not expressly refer to psychological health.[152]

However, there does appear to be some indication that many approaches to physical health and safety in the workplace might be exacerbating psychosocial harm.

---

[151] See for example the Model Work Health and Safety Regulations (https://www.safeworkaustralia.gov.au/sites/default/files/2023-08/model-whs-regulations-1_august_2023.pdf), Division 11.

[152] Education and Health Standing Committee. (2015). The impact of FIFO work practices on mental health: Final Report. Legislative Assembly. Perth: Parliament of Western Australia (**FIFO Review**).

In an inquiry into the possible impact of fly in/fly out work on "*mental health*" the Australian Medical Association identified that the way health and safety is managed can contribute to a "*distinct sense of entrapment*":

> *The AMA also expressed its concerns about this issue, noting that "[o]nerous rules, safety procedures and focus on achievement of production levels have been shown to create a distinct sense of entrapment in FIFO workers.*[153]

The inquiry drew, in some measure, on an earlier report[154] which also noted the adverse impact of safety and health management on psychological well-being. For example, "*[a]dhering to on-site safety rules*" was identified as a workplace stress.[155].

Interestingly, the Lifeline Report noted a sense of "*intimidation*" brought on by the number of rules and regulations associated with work on a mine, and:

> *This sense of intimidation was further mirrored in the outcomes of mining safety regulations which in theory were designed to care for workers but in practice led to inflexible regulation over genuine safety concerns.*[156]

Examples from the Lifeline Report include:

> *... a participant recalled a situation in which a worker handling heavy loads required an adhesive bandage but was unable to ask someone to get them for him because he had to fill out an accident report first (which he was unable to do mid-job); hence he had to carry on working without attending to his cuts. Alternatively, another example of the application of safety rules in an inflexible manner was illustrated when a group of workers were reprimanded for not wearing safety glasses on a 40 degree day even though they could not see from them due to excessive sweating. Hence, safety rules themselves were accepted as a necessary part of work but their implementation in an inflexible uniform manner created stress as workers felt their impact hindered their ability to conduct basic work tasks safely and/or without attracting rebuke. Hence, site rules and regulations could translate into arbitrary and*

---

[153] FIFO Review, p. 43.

[154] Sellenger Centre for Research in Law, Justice and Social Change. (2013). FIFO/DIDO Mental Health Research Report 2013. Perth: Lifeline WA (**Lifeline Report**).

[155] Lifeline Report, p.77.

[156] Lifeline Report, p.81.

> *punitive forms of punishment, which undermined participants' ability to fulfil jobs to their satisfaction and left them feeling insecure with their positions.*[157]

In part – perhaps a large part – formulating the workplace health and safety problem is the problem.

One of the difficulties I perceive in the application of metrics is the lack of definition around the workplace health and safety problem solution they are designed to evidence. It is all very well to require managers to spend time in the field having safety conversations – and measuring the number of those conversations – but what is the workplace health and safety problem that those conversations are trying to address?

Wicked problems have no stopping rules

When we solve a tame problem, we know when the job has been done. But when he is workplace health and safety solved? Arguably never.

I do not have the citation, and apologise in advance for any misattribution, but I believe it was Professor James Reason, in talking about root cause analysis who said that the root cause is the thing you are looking at when the time and the money runs out.

In many ways, this observation is symptomatic of the border workplace health and safety problems.

Constructing a processing facility on mine site is a difficult, expensive, and technically challenging *"problem"*. But we know when it has been completed. We do not know when a safety *"solution"* has been found.

Solutions to wicked problems are not true-or-false but good-or-bad

For most problems, no matter how complex, there are typically objective or at least known criteria that can be applied to decide whether a solution to the problem is correct. Workplace health and safety have no such criteria.

Technical experts can review a constructed bridge, for example, and objectively determine if it is designed properly The same cannot be said of public policy decisions relevant to the bridge, such as design or location. Further, the impact of a bridge may impact different parts of a community differently. For example, the location of a bridge might reduce travel time for commuters, but at the same time, divert traffic from

---

[157] Lifeline Report, p.81.

a commercial business, such as a fuel station. The true/false question in relation to the bridge looks different from different points of view.

The same is true of workplace health and safety. In a workplace health and safety environment, many parties have a stake in a workplace health and safety solution, and all are equally competent and equipped to form a view – from their perspective - about whether a workplace health and safety solution is good or bad. In many cases, those views may be wildly divergent.

A documented safe working procedure may be appealing at a management level of an organisation for a variety of reasons, include:

- apparent regulatory compliance;
- inexpensive;
- easy to evidence; and
- easy to disseminate.

From a supervisor and worker perspective, however, documented safe work procedures may not be fit for purpose – they may be perceived as irrelevant and unhelpful.

Yet in neither case can we say that documented safe working procedures are a correct *"solution"*:

> *... assessments of proposed solutions are expressed as "good" or "bad" or, more likely, as "better or worse" or "satisfying" or "good enough."*[158]

Typically, safe working procedures are a *"solution"* insofar as they are:

- what we have always done; or
- something we have historically invested in; or
- something we think the regulator expects to see.

There is no immediate and no ultimate test of a solution to a wicked problem

It is possible to test a solution for a tame problem to determine how successful it has been.

The same is not true of wicked problems, including workplace health and safety.

Even apparently successful solutions to the problem of workplace health and safety can generate unforeseen consequences over a long period of time which ultimately outweigh the advantages of any apparent earlier *"success"*.

---

[158] Wicked Problems, p. 163.

Safety as a wicked problem

As we have already seen, the fire and explosion that occurred at Esso's Longford Gas Plant in 1998 occurred in what was, for all intents and purposes, a well-run and safe facility. As was noted during the sentencing decision following the prosecution:

> *In presentation of material in the plea on behalf of Esso, learned senior counsel, Mr Titshall, referred to Esso's otherwise very good safety record. Credit should be given where credit is due. Mr Titshall elaborated that the foundation of Esso's safety management system was and is its Operations Integrity Management System, the manuals of which were in evidence. Mr Titshall rightly pointed out Esso's otherwise very good safety record in the petroleum industry. Between 1992 and 1996 Esso employees worked 12 and a half million employee hours without a single lost time injury, a technical definition involving fatality, permanent disability or time lost from work. He placed before me as Exhibit E1 data of that otherwise very good safety record. I acknowledge that record. He pointed out, rightly, that Esso is involved in heavy industry, including the gas plant concerned, and that that record stands to Esso's credit. He pointed out that since these matters of 25 September 1998, at Longford over 1.7 million work hours have been completed without any lost time injury. Further, the company has undertaken safety initiatives of numerous sorts which Mr Titshall elaborated: introduction of safety promoters, health and safety representatives, safety leader training courses, accident reporting systems, written expectations, safety awareness tests and other matters and general high standard job training and competency based assessments.*
>
> *Esso also has received a number of safety awards. It has a five star rating award from the National Safety Council in 1991, APIA safety awards for 1994, 1995, 1996, 1999 and 2000, being the best safety performance of large companies, and the Fluor Daniel corporate tri-star award for 100,000 hours accident free in 1999. It also has other awards and commendable safety records including 100,000 mishap-free flying hours of helicopters to platforms. Credit there is properly given to Esso for its otherwise very good safety record.*[159]

Longford is not the only example of an organisation with seemingly good safety performance to have a catastrophic workplace accident and

---

[159]　*Director of Public Prosecutions v Esso Australia Pty Ltd* [2001] VSC 263, [29] – [30].

the subsequent enquiries to reveal deep flaws in the way workplace health and safety was managed. Notwithstanding the *"otherwise very good safety record"* the Royal Commission into the disaster was highly critical of the company's management of safety. For example:

> *Reliance placed by Esso on its OIMS for the safe operation of the plant was misplaced. The accident on 25 September 1998 demonstrated in itself, that important components of Esso's system of management were either defective or not implemented. If the implementation of OIMS by Esso was to be measured by the adequacy of its operating procedures, they were deficient and failed to conform with the ECI Upstream Guidelines or with the OIMS Systems Manual. If it was to be measured by reference to the actions and decisions of those persons who were attempting to resolve the process upsets on 25 September 1998, they were also deficient. The deficiencies were in the manner in which Esso dealt with the acquisition and retention of knowledge. This involved its training system, its operating procedures, its documentation and data system and its communication system.[160]*

A similar example can be found, for example, in the inquiry into the 20 April 2010 Deepwater Horizon disaster in the Gulf of Mexico. Inquiries into this disaster revealed that Deepwater Horizon drilling rig involved in the disaster had gone 7 years without a lost time injury on the facility, yet again as with Longford, enquiries were highly critical of the management of safety on the facility:

> *Decision making processes at Macondo did not adequately ensure that personnel fully considered the risks created by time- and money-saving decisions. Whether purposeful or not, many of the decisions that BP, Halliburton, and Transocean made that increased the risk of the Macondo blowout clearly saved those companies significant time (and money).*
>
> *There is nothing inherently wrong with choosing a less-costly or less-time-consuming alternative—as long as it is proven to be equally safe. The problem is that, at least in regard to BP's Macondo team, there appears to have been no formal system for ensuring that alternative procedures were in fact equally safe. None of BP's (or the other companies') decisions in Figure 4.10 appear to have been subject to a comprehensive and systematic risk-analysis,*

---

[160] Longford Royal Commission at [13.42]

> *peer-review, or management of change process. The*
> *evidence now available does not show that the BP team*
> *members (or other companies' personnel) responsible for*
> *these decisions conducted any sort of formal analysis to*
> *assess the relative riskiness of available alternatives.*[161]

Workplace health and safety is not a problem to be *"solved"*. We can tackle it, we can try to tame it, but always recognising that workplace health and safety is continually in motion and there is no guarantee that anything successfully implemented today will work tomorrow, or indeed may be sowing the seeds for potential disaster in the future.

Every solution to a wicked problem is a "one-shot operation"

Each new attempt to solve workplace health and safety often involves significant philosophical shifts in thinking, or at least substantial financial inputs and organisational effort. Further, once a safety initiative has been implemented, it is notoriously difficult to remove, even if they provide no useful benefit to workplace health and safety, or indeed undermine workplace health and safety.

Problematically, and in light of the other characteristics of wicked problems already described, the solution necessarily involves trade-offs – typically based on how the organisation has defined the problem of workplace health and safety in the first place. No safety solution, however well intended, will definitively achieve workplace health and safety because of the characteristics described above, which means the *"product"* will always be a less than perfect solution and will always require workarounds for the organisation, and individuals within it, to achieve their goals.

The health and safety industry is replete with productised safety initiatives, for example:

- incident investigation methodology;
- behavioural-based safety programs;
- *"safety conversations"* programs;
- "safety leadership" programs;
- supervisor training programs;
- outsourced, online induction programs; and
- a variety of safety software programs and databases.

Once any of these programs have been introduced into an organisation, they tend to become embedded and perpetuate. Safety

---

[161] Deepwater Report, p. 125

initiatives are not introduced on a *"trial"* basis with any meaningful assessment of their usefulness or effectiveness in improving workplace health and safety. The safety decisionmaker does not get the option of running a safety leadership program across the organisation and then going to the chief executive officer or the board to replace the program.

However, these problems are not limited to organisational or micro-level safety initiatives. National policy initiatives for workplace health and safety, most often reflected in legislation, also have a significant bearing on organisational responses to the management of workplace health and safety, and legislation once installed is extraordinarily difficult to unwind.

Australia, as an example, has proceeded strongly down the path of retributive justice in its workplace health and safety legislation. This model of legislation is based on multi-million-dollar fines and terms of life imprisonment for individuals in some jurisdictions.[162] The poster child of this approach to workplace health and safety legislation is the imposition in most Australian jurisdictions of an offence of industrial manslaughter.[163]

The evidence that a system of retributive justice with such significant penalties will have any meaningful effect in the context of workplace health and safety is slim to non-existent. Yet all jurisdictions in Australia have adopted this approach.

I have never been a fan of the notion of industrial manslaughter,[164] and in my view the consequences of the retributive justice approach were obvious before the legislation was introduced. Indeed, one of those consequences was brought to light in a 2023 inquiry into fatalities in the agricultural industry in Western Australia:[165]

> *The new industrial manslaughter provisions and the new penalties have been a double-edged sword. On one side, they have raised awareness of safety in agriculture in an unprecedented way and they have caused many farmers to seek advice and assistance from consultants and training organisations.*
>
> *It has been reported by farmers that the quality of service provided by those consultants and training organisations*

---

162 *Work Health and Safety (National Uniform Legislation) Act 2011* (NT), section 34B.
163 See for example: *Work Health and Safety Act 2022* (WA), section 30A.
164 https://www.waylandlegal.com.au/post/why-i-do-not-support-industrial-manslaughter
165 Scott. P. (2023) *Inquiry into the agricultural industry in Western Australia*: Report to the WorkSafe Commissioner. Government of Western Australia WorkSafe Commissioner. (**WorkSafe Agricultural Inquiry**)

> *ranges from excellent to poor. Farmers are confused and concerned about making a good choice of adviser, and about a significant cost in obtaining advice and assistance.*
>
> *The other edge of the sword is that these provisions have been described as a "cudgel" and have raised fear, panic and alarm. There has been a deal of scaremongering amongst a range of people and organisations. They have used the prospect of imprisonment and large fines, firstly, to oppose the introduction of the legislation, and secondly, to tout for business.*
>
> *That fear adds to the anxiety many farmers already have at the prospect of dealing with the regulator, through inspectors. Many have expressed that fear during community engagement processes during this Inquiry and have cited their own and others' bad experiences in dealing with inspectors in the past. It means many farmers, as they have said, "keep their heads below the parapet" and avoid engagement with the regulator. This also means that they do not seek assistance or advice from the regulator because they do not wish to draw attention to themselves.*[166]

Moreover, there does not appear to be any indication that the model of retributive justice is leading to better health and safety outcomes across Australia. Based on data published by Safe Work Australia,[167] there does not appear to be any significant statistical difference between fatality rates pre-and post the introduction of work health and safety legislation for most jurisdictions, nor any significant statistical difference between jurisdictions that adopted work health and safety legislation and those that did not.[168]

So where does this leave us? If workplace fatality rates in Australia remain the same, or get worse, or fluctuate over time, how do we proceed? It seems almost inconceivable that any health and safety lobby group would be prepared to stand up and say retributive justice does not work and we need to unwind our system of regulation. So, do we double down? Is the next step *"industrial murder"*?

---

[166] WorkSafe Agricultural Inquiry, pp. 44 – 45,

[167] https://data.safeworkaustralia.gov.au/interactive-data

[168] At the time of writing, Victoria has not adopted work health and safety legislation. Western Australia only adopted work health and safety legislation in March 2022.

Year	Australian Capital Territory	New South Wales	Northern Territory	Queensland	South Australia	Tasmania	Victoria	Western Australia
Fatality rate (fatalities per 100,000 workers)								
2003	0.6	2.7	4.1	3.2	1.8	8.2	2.3	2.9
2004	1.7	2.4	13.3	3.1	2.7	6.1	2.8	3.7
2005	0.5	2.9	5.2	3.6	2.4	3.6	1.7	2.2
2006	1	2.9	6	3	2.7	4.5	2.7	2.1
2007	0.5	2.6	9.3	3.7	1.3	4.8	2.7	4
2008	0	2.5	8.1	3.5	1.9	3.8	1.8	3.7
2009	1	1.9	5	3.1	2.4	6.4	1.9	2.8
2010	0.5	1.9	5	2.2	2.5	2.9	1.8	2.6
2011	0.5	1.7	5.8	2.7	2.2	3.8	1.7	1.9
2012	1.4	2.4	7.1	2.5	1.6	2.6	1.2	1.9
2013	0.5	1.5	3.1	2.4	1.9	3.5	1.2	2.4
2014	0	1.6	3	2.2	1.2	3.4	1.5	1.9
2015	0	1.7	1.5	2.2	1.2	2.5	1.3	3.2
2016	0.5	1.4	3	1.9	2.6	2.5	1.2	1.4
2017	0.4	1.6	5.1	1.8	1.7	2	1.1	1.6
2018	0.4	1.2	2.2	1.6	1.1	0.4	1	0.8
2019	0	1.6	5.4	1.6	1.8	2.4	1	1.6
2020	0.8	1.3	4.6	1.4	1.3	3.2	1.5	2.1

A regulatory model based on retributive justice is clearly a *"one-shot"* operation. It is not a philosophy of workplace health and safety that is easily stepped back, and the health and safety industry, including its most important constituents – workers – will need to deal with the consequences and trade-offs of this social policy decision for (in all likelihood) decades to come.

Wicked problems do not have an enumerable set of potential solutions

Both problems and solutions are difficult to define when dealing with a wicked problem, and as we have seen from the discussion so far this is true of workplace health and safety.

Most complex problems have a finite set of rules or solutions, often bounded by *"hard"* sciences such as physics, mathematics, or chemistry, but the broader question of workplace health and safety does not have such boundaries. It is also less clear what is *"permissible"* in terms of solutions. Is it *"permissible"* to reduce injury rates by redefining what qualifies as a *"lost time"* injury?

As the authors of the paper state:

> *In such fields of ill-defined problems and hence ill-defined solutions, the set of feasible plans of action relies on realistic judgement, capability to appraise "exotic" ideas and on the amount of trust and credibility between planner and clientele that will lead to the conclusion, "okay let us try that."* [169]

---

[169] Wicked Problems, p. 164.

And very often our workplace health and safety solutions are what organisations are familiar with. It is not unheard of (and perhaps not uncommon) for a senior manager come into a new organisation to bring workplace health and safety ideas and strategies from the old organisation based purely on their personal view that those strategies were previously successful. As we have seen through this discussion on wicked problems that is a very dangerous assumption to make, but familiarity with workplace health and safety strategies often leads to their adoption.

It is, of course, difficult to test some of our ideas for safety. For example, would be ethical to run a double-blind study whereby a portion of the workforce receives a workplace health and safety induction, and a portion of the workforce does not, to test the efficacy of inductions? I suspect not.

Every wicked problem is essentially unique

In the article, the authors note that while there may be apparent similarities amongst wicked prob can never be certain *"that the particulars of the problem do not override its commonalities with other problems already deal with."*[170] by way of example they say:

> *The conditions in a city constructing a subway may look similar to the conditions in San Francisco, say; but planners would be ill-advised to transfer the San Francisco solutions directly. Differences in commuter habits or residential patterns may far outweigh similarities in subway layout, downtown layout and the rest. In the more complex world of social policy planning, every situation is likely to be one-of-a-kind. If we are right about that, the direct transference of the physical science and engineering thoughtways into social policy might be dysfunctional, i.e. positively harmful. "Solutions" might be applied to seemingly familiar problems which are quite incompatible with them.[171]*

I do not think this juxtaposition would come as a surprise to anybody working at the operational end of workplace health and safety. The idea that we can simply translate a mechanic or process that has been *"successfully"* applied in one industry to another seems to be powerfully attractive in the health and safety industry, and many people *"borrow"* safety ideas and apply them in a like for like manner in a new

---

[170] Wicked Problems, p. 165.
[171] Wicked Problems, p. 165.

organisation. This level of borrowing extends all the way to things as specific as safe work procedures indeed, it is not uncommon to find organisations operating with safe working procedures which still include the name of the organisation from which it was borrowed.

An example of borrowing that has become somewhat problematic in the Australian context are safe work method statements. Safe work method statements (colloquially referred to as *"swims"*) are a requirement under work health and safety legislation and they are only required in relation to 18 specifically regulated high risk construction activities, including construction work that:

- involves a risk of a person falling more than 2 m;
- involves, was likely to involve, the disturbance of asbestos;
- is carried out in an area at a workplace in which there is any movement of powered mobile plant; or
- is carried out in or near water or other liquid that involves a risk of drowning.

Problematically, in my view safe work method statements have been adopted for a whole range of activities for which they were never intended. I have seen organisations that have developed safe work method statements for tasks such as carrying boxes, climbing over fences on farms, and changing light globes. In my experience this general adoption of the safe work method statement model for work that it was never designed for has created two problems.

First, it has led to the creation of documented procedures for work activities simply do not need them.

Second, and in my view a more concerning issue, is that safe work method statements have become despised in many workplaces, becoming just another bureaucratic process that workers have to deal with before they can get on with their work and losing any remnant of criticality they might once have had. If I have to complete and follow a safe work method statement to change a light globe, it is not unforeseeable that workers would come to see the safe work method statement process as trivial.

If, on the other hand, we were to limit safe work method statements to their intended purpose – <u>high risk</u> construction work - then it would seem more likely they would be treated with the seriousness they should.

Every wicked problem can be considered to be a symptom of another problem

A common trope in the new view of safety is that worker behaviour is not the problem – it is an expression of the problem. Based on that perspective, the role of work health and safety management is not to "*fix*" the worker, but rather to fix the environment within which they operate.

While I think this concept is too binary it does have some merit provided the right balance can be found between the worker and the environment. However, for the purpose of this discussion it is illustrative of the dilemma of cause and effect in safety.

At an organisational level, causal chains in workplace health and safety can be infinitely long. For example, if a worker is involved in an incident where they did not comply with the procedure is the problem with:

- The procedure?
- The training on the procedure?
- The attitude of the worker?
- External factors, such as time or resource constraints?

If the problem is with the procedure, is it a problem with the procedure broadly or a problem with the procedure in the context of the specific task at the specific time?

What if the worker has poor literacy? Is this accounted for in our training?

Does poor worker literacy indicate a problem in our recruitment processes?

But when we step back further away from organisational process there are broader questions about other factors which might impact on workplace health and safety. For example, have we made workplaces too safe so that young workers do not know how to recognise risk?

Should workplace safety be taught in schools so that workers come to the workforce with an understanding of workplace risk?

Can workplace health and safety requirements be applied fairly between large and small organisations having regard to the economic resources available?

Do insecure employment arrangements (subcontracting, casualisation of workforces, the gig economy) lead to less safe workplaces?

Of course, many of the factors which may affect workplace health and safety are beyond the control of the workplace. But at the same time, we need to be careful that we are not simply moving around our organisations fixing "*symptoms*", and we need to define the "*problem*" of workplace health and safety at a high enough level to address the broader symptoms in the organisation.

The choice of explanation determines the nature of the problems resolution

There are many explanations for the problem of workplace health and safety - just look at the constant debate surrounding the new view of safety. The advocates of different explanations for the problem of workplace health and safety appear to be retreating further and further into their own echo chambers, and unlike much of the scientific or engineering communities there is no set of rules or a procedure to determine the correct explanation for the problem of workplace health and safety, or even what combination of various explanations might best explain the problem.

The choice of explanation of the problem of workplace health and safety, however, appears to align closely with the various proponents' worldview, or area of technical expertise:

> *That is to say, the choice of explanation is arbitrary in the logical sense. In actuality, attitudinal criteria guide the choice. People choose those explanations which are most plausible to them. Somewhat but not much exaggerated, you might say that everybody picks the explanation of a discrepancy which fits his intentions best and which conforms to the action-prospects that are available to him. The analyst's "worldview" is the strongest determining factor in explaining a discrepancy and, therefore, in resolving a wicked problem.*[172]

I have heard a nuclear technician coming out of the US Navy describe safety as a "*physics problem*", and from their point of view, that makes perfect sense. However, it does not account for the rapidly expanding and complex problem of "*psychosocial risk*".

More than any other area in my experience, the health and safety industry seem to attract the widest collection of worldviews which, unfortunately, appear to operate in opposition to each other rather than collaboratively. Consider the moment the following worldviews which appear across the spectrum of the health and safety industry:

- the tertiary qualified health and safety manager;

---

[172] Wicked Problems, p. 166.

- the safety manager who has come up through the ranks with operational experience;
- the engineer;
- the sociologist;
- the psychologist;
- the occupational hygienist; or
- the technical expert in any number of specific fields.[173]

I have no doubt that I have missed other categories of worldviews that populate the workplace health and safety environment.

And at no point do I seek to exclude myself from the dilemma of a particular worldview. Indeed, I accept that this book is being written from the worldview of a lawyer. But I take comfort in sharing my worldview from the fact that:

- my worldview is seen by the health and safety industry as the minimum standard, and to the extent that this position is accepted, all worldviews populating the health and safety industry should have at least some interest in achieving the minimum standard; and
- unlike the rest of the health and safety industry, there are rules and procedures to determine, if not the correct explanation for the problem of workplace health and safety, at least whether the problem has been dealt with satisfactorily – that is, the prosecution of individuals and organisations through the judicial system.

The planner has no right to be wrong

From a societal perspective, organisations have no right to be mistaken in their workplace health and safety strategies.

While workplace health and safety performance in most industrialised, Western nations at least, has improved remarkably over the last 30 or 40 years, most industrial accidents and certainly workplace fatalities, still generate significant levels of public outrage. Organisations are often unjustly and harshly criticised following workplace accidents, with allegations that the organisation did not do enough to care for their people, or that they put commercial benefits before the well-being of their workers – production before safety.

---

[173] To name but a few, lifting operations, chemicals, explosives, asbestos, dangerous goods generally, working at heights, confined spaces, fire safety risk, fatigue - and on it goes.

I do not doubt that there are recalcitrant employers who do not pay sufficient attention to safety. But whether that is because they do not *"care"* about safety, or because they lack sufficient understanding of how to manage safety, or they lack the resources to manage safety, or they lack the wherewithal (or a combination of all those things) is hard to say.

What does seem to be the case, however, is that our genuine best endeavours are not sufficient if something goes wrong.

We have created an unhelpful fiction that all accidents are preventable, when the true position is more likely that all accidents were preventable with the benefit of hindsight.

Workplace health and safety we are not entitled to do our best – we must be right all the time.

Safety as a wicked problem

PART 6
ON METRICS

The statistical information provided to the board on health and safety comprised mainly personal injury rates and time lost through accidents ... The information gave the board some insight but was not much help in assessing the risks of a catastrophic event faced by high hazard industries. ... The board appears to have received no information proving the effectiveness of crucial systems such as gas monitoring and ventilation.[174]

---

[174] Pike River, p. 53.

I have already touched on some of the problems associated with metrics used to measure safety in organisations and in this part of the book, I want to expand on those issues and explain why I do not think metrics are useful.

To be clear, when I say I do not think metrics are useful, I am arguing that both lead and lag indicators:

- do not tell us anything meaningful about the state of safety in an organisation; and
- do not provide anything helpful in the event of a prosecution under health and safety legislation.

I would also point out that except where I reference specific research, the observations on metrics described below are based on:

- my observations and experiences dealing with and advising clients over the years; and
- my personal involvement in legal proceedings as well as the judgements of courts and findings of inquiries.

While I am critical of the current state of health and safety metrics, and the ability of commonly used health and safety metrics to tell us very much at all about the state of workplace health and safety, I am not arguing that those concerns are universal and that all health and safety metrics "*fail*" all the time and in every organisation. What I would say, however, is that the criticism of health and safety metrics described below is common enough in my experience to warrant the attention of organisations.

Health and safety metrics are based on certain (often untested) assumptions and are subject to organisational corruption. In these circumstances, it is my view that it is incumbent on organisations to not simply assume that their health and safety metrics are valid, but to ask the "*what if*" question – what if the information underpinning our workplace health and safety metrics is not valid – and then actively test their health and safety metrics to positively prove their validity.

However, even if our workplace health and safety metrics are valid and not undermined by assumption or organisational corruption that I will describe below, they still will not be evidence that an organisation is meeting its legal obligations. Without more, current workplace health and safety metrics do not evidence that an organisation has "*proper systems*" to manage the work health and safety hazards in the business, or that those systems are in place or effective.

LAG INDICATORS

There has been a significant amount of commentary about the inability of "*lag*" indicators – predominantly injury rate data, including measures of "*Lost Time*" injuries and "*recordable*" injuries – to inform an organisation about the state of workplace health and safety within its business.

A recent paper *The Statistical Invalidity of TRIR as a Measure of Safety Performance*[175] concluded that:

- there is no discernible association between Total Recordable Injury Rate (**TRIR**) and fatalities;
- the occurrence of recordable injuries is almost entirely random;
- in nearly every practical circumstance, it is statistically invalid to use TRIR to compare companies, business units, projects, or teams.[176]

Another recent paper, *A capacity index to replace a flawed incident based metrics for worker safety*[177] also described several problems with the use of incident based metrics as a measure of safety, stating that "*[l]ow numbers of injuries are not predictive of fatalities or accidents, so they do not constitute a safety measure*".

The problems with personal injury rate data have also been called out in several major accident inquiries. For example, the Pike River Royal Commission observed:

> *The statistical information provided to the board on health and safety comprised mainly personal injury rates and time lost through accidents ... The information gave the board some insight but was not much help in assessing the risks of a catastrophic event faced by high hazard industries. ...*

---

[175] Quashne M, Michael R., Bradley A. MacLean B and Quinn E. (2020) "The Statistical Invalidity of TRIR as a Measure of Safety Performance." Construction Safety Research Alliance. (**TRIR Paper**)

[176] Measures of safety based on injury rate data can vary between companies and jurisdictions. In the TRIR Paper, the authors state that "*Total recordable incident rate (TRIR) has been used as the primary measure of safety performance for nearly 50 years. Simply, TRIR is the rate at which a company experiences an OSHA-recordable incident, scaled per 200,000 worker hours. TRIR is based upon a standard definition of a "recordable" incident that was created and institutionalized in the recordkeeping requirements of the Occupational Safety and Health Act of 1970 (US Bureau of Labor Statistics 2019). According to the general criteria, an incident is recordable if it results in work-related injury or illness involving loss of consciousness or requiring medical treatment beyond first aid, days away from work, restricted work, or transfer to another job (US Department of Labor 2010).*", P. 2

[177] Dekker, S.W.A. and Tooma, M. (2022), A capacity index to replace flawed incident-based metrics for worker safety. International Labour Review, 161: 375-393. https://doi.org/10.1111/ilr.12210 (**Due Diligence Index**).

The board appears to have received no information proving the effectiveness of crucial systems such as gas monitoring and ventilation.[178]

The Baker Panel Review similarly observed:

Based on its review, the Panel believes that BP has not provided effective process safety leadership and has not adequately established process safety as a core value across all its five U.S. refineries. While BP has an aspirational goal of "no accidents, no harm to people," BP has not provided effective leadership in making certain its management and U.S. refining workforce understand what is expected of them regarding process safety performance. BP has emphasized personal safety in recent years and has achieved significant improvement in personal safety performance, but BP did not emphasize process safety. BP mistakenly interpreted improving personal injury rates as an indication of acceptable process safety performance at its U.S. refineries. BP's reliance on this data, combined with an inadequate process safety understanding, created a false sense of confidence that BP was properly addressing process safety risks.[179]

Finally, the Deepwater Report noted:

BP has proclaimed the importance of safety for its vast worldwide operations. "Our goal of 'no accidents, no harm to people and no damage to the environment' is fundamental to BP's activities," stated the company's Sustainability Review 2009. "We work to achieve this through consistent management processes, ongoing training programmes, rigorous risk management and a culture of continuous improvement." It added that "creating a safe and healthy working environment is essential for our success. Since 1999, injury rates and spills have reduced by approximately 75%.

Yet despite the improvement in injury and spill rates during that decade, BP has caused a number of disastrous or potentially disastrous workplace incidents that suggest its approach to managing safety has been on individual worker occupational safety but not on process safety. These incidents and subsequent analyses indicate that the company does not have consistent and reliable risk-management processes—and thus has been unable to meet

---

[178] Pike River, p. 53.
[179] Baker Panel Review, p. 14.

> *its professed commitment to safety. BP's safety lapses have been chronic.*[180]

The lesson from these inquiries is that, not only does injury rate data not provide any real insight into the state of workplace health and safety management in an organisation, but importantly, focusing on personal injury rates can also distract an organisation from the critical risks in the business.

It might also be worth reflecting that we do not have unlimited resources of time and effort in an organisation, and that every moment spent chasing down, classifying, counting, collating, and reporting on injury rates – a measure that seemingly, self-evidently, does not contribute to safety in workplaces, is time we do not spend on other, more value adding processes.

From a legal risk management perspective, it is also worth considering the value of injury rate data in defending an organisation after a workplace accident. What evidence does an industry-leading industry rate performance play in demonstrating that an organisation was meeting its legal obligations? For all practical purposes, none.

If a worker falls from height at work and dies, there is nothing in an organisation's injury rate target that provides any insight into whether the organisation had proper systems to manage the risk of falls in the workplace, and whether, or to what extent, they systems were implemented and effective. If you do not accept that position, read any work health and safety prosecution decision. Injury rate data is not referred to, much less relied on by the defence.

I have used injury rate data in work health and safety prosecutions, but only by way of arguing for a mitigation of penalty.

In basic terms, when a company is convicted of an offence under work health and safety legislation. The judge will decide a starting point for the penalty based on the objective seriousness of the offence. The penalty will then be adjusted based on any aggravating or mitigating circumstances. By way of example, an early plea of guilty to a charge is a significant mitigating factor. Penalties will often be reduced by up to 25% of what would otherwise be imposed, based on an early plea of guilty. Another factor in mitigation is whether the organisation took its obligations for workplace health and safety seriously and it is in this area that injury rate data could be used.

---

[180] Deepwater Report, p. 218.

Generally, in arguing for mitigation, a company will try and demonstrate that it took its responsibilities for safety seriously, and point to factors such as:

- extensive safety systems;
- the size of the organisation's safety budget;
- the structure of the safety organisation; or any applicable safety awards or accreditations.

If an organisation's injury rate data is objectively "*good*", for example lower than the industry standard rate published by the regulator, then the company may include this fact as part of a broader argument that they took their workplace health and safety responsibilities seriously.

This, then, it seems to me is the very limited role injury rate data can play in providing evidence that workplace health and safety is well-managed.

However, there may be some opportunities to use injury rate data to prompt questions or provide signposts to where the organisation might need to pay attention. It may be that if we direct our energy to analysing our incidents, – as opposed to classifying them – they might reveal trends or developments that warrant further investigations or interventions. For example, analysis of workplace injuries might reveal:

- trends in certain types of injuries, such as hand or back injuries;
- spikes of injuries at certain times of year, for example, prior to Christmas; or
- spikes in injuries in certain geographic locations or certain parts of the business.

Changes in injury rate data (up or down) may or may not signify anything of importance or any issues with the workplace health and safety management systems, but it could provide a prompt to ask questions.

One final point on injury rate data as an indicator of safety performance, is the extent to which it is extensively used in contractor selection processes. Many organisations, when selecting contractors, will ask the contractor to provide information about their injury rate data, and then track the injury rate data during the life of the contract. I have seen contracts which include injury rate data as a key performance indicator as part of the contract.

This is problematic in at least two ways. First as both the Due Diligence Index and the TRIR paper point out, injury rate data is not a valid method to compare organisational safety performance. It would be very hard for organisations to argue that a contractors injury rate data is a valid reflection of their safety performance or the efficacy of their work health and safety management processes.

However, I think reliance on injury rate data as a measure of contractor performance goes beyond being simply problematic and has the potential to be dangerous. If contractor selection and performance is based on or measured against injury rate data, then we run the very real risk of contractors consciously or unconsciously *"manipulating"* injury rate data to either win jobs, or to meet contractual requirements. The idea that contractual requirements can override a contractor's approach to health and safety management is not a new idea, and it is one that has manifested itself in legal proceedings.

In the Ferro Con decision,[181] a worker was killed on a construction project when a 14 m beam being lifted by a crane slipped, fell, and hit the worker. The company, Ferro Con, was a subcontractor engaged in the construction of a desalination plant.

The court was critical of the way Fero Con approached workplace health and safety management on the project:

> *At the day's pre-start toolbox meeting each employee was required to sign a "cover sheet" to the general JSA to acknowledge they were aware of it. Each employee was also required to sign a general safety awareness document called a START card. This is an acronym for Stop, Think, Assess, Review and Talk. Whilst the START cards had space for specific hazard control measures to be added, nothing was noted about this lifting job. As described by the prosecutor, the signings were primarily treated by both Ferro Con and the employees as a 'tick and flick' exercise.[182]*

However, the court went on to describe that one of the problems with the way Ferro Con managed workplace health and safety, was that the management was primarily concerned to comply with contractual requirements rather than managing foreseeable workplace health and safety risks:

> *As indicated, a cover sheet to the structural steel erection JSA was signed daily, largely as a perfunctory exercise to fulfil Adelaide Aqua's requirements.*
>
> *No detailed JSA's for different types of lifts, or lift plans, were required by Adelaide Aqua. Ferro Con took its cue for*

---

¹⁸¹ *Hillman v Ferro Con (SA) Pty Ltd (in liquidation) and Anor* [2013] SAIRC 22 (**Ferro Con**).

¹⁸² Ferro Con, [15].

> *the level of safety planning it would use in its work from Adelaide Aqua, and not from the foreseeable hazards of its work activities. Ferro Con was more focussed on complying with contractual requirements than taking all reasonably practicable steps to minimise the foreseeable hazards its business created.*[183]

Most people who have been involved with contractor safety management at an operational level would recognise this, or similar phenomena. If you ask a contractor to provide something to win a contract or to meet contractual key performance indicators, it is very likely that the contractor will give it to you. If that *"something"* is injury rate data, then in all likelihood, the contractor will produce a number that is at or below the required number.

I think in those circumstances injury rate data goes beyond being unhelpful and uninformative to being potentially dangerous.

LEAD INDICATORS

The difficulties with lead indicators appear to me to be both structural and that they are not fit for purpose.

Structurally, lead indicators are based on important assumptions and are subject to organisational or institutional corruption which I have discussed previously and will explore in more detail below.

I will discuss examples of underpinning assumptions in the sections below, but fundamentally my concern is that the assumptions on which lead indicators rely are not overt or discussed, much less properly tested. The failure to properly test the assumptions underpinning lead indicators fundamentally undermines any credibility they might have as an indicator of workplace health and safety.

Lead indicators are also not fit for purpose. At their highest they may give us some confidence that some activity is occurring which has some relationship to an element of workplace health and safety. The completion of these activities, no matter how well performed, can never be an indication of the overall state of workplace health and safety in an organisation – at best it is an indication that some small part of the overall workplace health and safety picture is being given close attention.

Finally, and again from my legal perspective, I think it is worth noting that lead indicators have no value in legal proceedings. When you look to the history of prosecutions under health and safety legislation in Australia, you will not find any observations or comments by the court

---

[183] Ferro Con, [43] – [44].

on an organisation's lead safety indicators. You will not find any references in the courts judgements of submissions made by defence counsel pointing to an organisation's lead health and safety indicators as evidence that their workplaces were *"safe"*, or that the lead indicators were somehow evidence that the organisation was doing everything reasonably practicable to manage the hazards in the business.

Below, I have provided a more detailed analysis of some common workplace health and safety lead indicators to illustrate the concerns described above.

Management Conversations

A common indicator used to assess workplace health and safety is some measure of management interaction with the workforce. They are often described in terms such as *"leadership observations"* or *"safety conversations"* or *"safety observations"*. A modern variant of this theme are the *"4Ds"*, a conversation methodology based on asking questions around:

- when do something we have to do the safety seem "*dumb*";
- when things seem dangerous;
- when something different; and
- when is something difficult to do or do well.[184]

The 4Ds methodology as I understand it, is directed to an open inquiry and trying to understand the gap between what is commonly referred to as Work-As-Imagined and Work-As-Done,[185] but the methodology is still fundamentally directed at understanding the management of workplace health and safety at the frontline.

While recognising there are philosophical and structural differences between these different *"observational"* methodologies, for ease of reference in this section of the book I will refer to these broadly as *"Management Conversations"*.

As mentioned above, like all lead indicators, Management Conversations are underpinned by assumptions and face the potential threat of corruption, both of which if left untested, undermine the credibility of Management Conversations as an indicator of workplace health and safety. Some of the assumptions that must necessarily underpin any program of Management Conversations are:

---

[184] Sutton. B, Lyth. J, Robinson. B, Bryant. J. (2023). 4Ds for HOP and Learning Teams: A practical how-to guide to learn from everyday work, critical and dynamic risks with the 4Ds. Learning Teams Inc. (**4Ds**), pp. 37 – 39, 47 - 56.
[185] 4Ds, pp. 152 – 153.

- *Competence*: How can organisations be sure that its managers are competent to hold work health and safety conversations and not disengage the workers?
- *Understanding – safety*: How can organisations be confident that managers understand safety generally and the safety expectations of the organisation specifically?
- *Understanding – systems*: How can organisations be confident that managers understand the work health and safety management systems of the organisation sufficiently to identify if they have been complied with, or to discuss the application of those systems with workers?
- ***Work is genuinely represented***: How confident is the organisation that when managers are having Conversations with workers, the work they are observing genuinely represents the way the work is normally performed, and do managers have enough understanding of the way that the organisation thinks work is performed (work as imagined) to understand if there is a difference?
- ***Consistency of management messages***: How does the organisation get assurance that Management Conversations are consistent, and that different messages or different expectations are not being created in different parts of the organisation?

To a large extent, it is possible that all of these assumptions can be tested, and appropriate measures put in place to ensure that personnel conducting Management Conversations have a level of competence and understanding to enable them to hold a useful Management Conversation. However, we must also consider the very real phenomena of organisational corruption in the context of Management Conversations.

It does seem to me that to a large extent a primary driver of organisational corruption that undermines Management Conversations is the application of a metric to measure the number of Conversations happening.

Two examples of organisational corruption of Management Conversations that I have seen are *"timeliness"* and *"geography"*.

In terms of timeliness, it is common to observe the majority of Management Conversations occurring very close to the reporting deadline. So, for example, in one organisation I worked with more than 80% of Management Conversations regularly occurred in the last week of the month before the end of month *"cut off"* for the health and safety report. This compressed timeframe for Management Conversations limited the potential effectiveness of the process. For example, cramming multiple Management Conversations into a week before reports were due:

- Undermine the credibility of the whole process and emphasised to workers and management alike that the Conversation was just a compliance exercise to meet a target.
- Missed entire parts of the workforce due to the rosters in place, and conversely, bombarded other parts of the workforce with multiple Conversations missing out on potential variations of opinions, while at the same time disengaging an entire segment of the workplace (the *"always talked to"* group) from the process.
- Missed potential opportunities to pick up on weak signals as attitudes or behaviours shifted or developed over the entire month – something that is less likely to be evident over the period of a week.

The geography question essentially means that Management Conversations occur in a place that is geographically convenient for the manager. The geography question often occurs in conjunction with the timeliness question, but I have seen examples of its operating independently.

In one case, for managers working in the main administration office on a mine site, more than 70% of their Management Conversations occurred at a vehicle maintenance workshop that was only 200m from the administration building. No doubt convenient for the managers, but very limited in terms of the insight into workplace health and safety – or any other insights – that might be gained from the Management Conversations.

Of course, none of these characteristics – or any other assumptions or potentially corrupting influences – are identified or made overt in the metric. The metric is simply presented as a number, or more commonly some sort of traffic light indicator (green for good, amber for okay, red for bad), but no information that would allow an insight into the quality or efficacy of the Management Conversations – not just as a measure of workplace health and safety but as a management exercise in itself – is ever surfaced. Critical underlying questions remain unasked and unanswered.

I am not suggesting for a moment that organisations who engage in a program of Management Conversations are wasting their time.

On Metrics

Obviously, there are significant benefits from having executive management able to engage in a meaningful way with the rest of the organisation and it is quite likely that many of these Management Conversations do reveal important safety information and do give executive managers some useful insight into the operations of the business generally, and the presence and management of health and safety hazards and risks specifically.

At the same time, however, it must be recognised that Management Conversations have the potential, not just to fail to meet their specific objectives, but to positively undermine safety because of the nature of the interactions and to create an illusion of safety by being presented as a successful activity in monthly health and safety reports. The challenge for organisations that want to rely on Management Conversations as a measure of workplace health and safety performance is to recognise and understand the assumptions that underpin their program of Management Conversations, and to recognise the potential for organisational corruption, and then to make those issues of assumption and corruption overt and test and challenge the process of Management Conversations having regard to those issues to ensure the integrity of the process.

But even if we are prepared to invest the time and effort into understanding the assumptions and potential corruption of our program of Management Conversations, what does a successful, well conducted program of Management Conversations actually tell us about the state of workplace health and safety in our organisation? Arguably, very little.

From a legal risk management perspective there are two key themes that run in parallel.

First, is the reasonably practicable question; does the organisation have proper systems to manage the workplace health and safety hazards in the business and are those systems implemented and effective.

The second theme is "*criticality*".

Many cases call out the failure by organisations to address "*critical*", or "*important*", or "*fundamental*" workplace health and safety issues.

We see this reflected in the Pike River Royal Commission, where the Royal Commission observed that the "*board appears to have received no information proving the effectiveness of crucial systems such as gas monitoring and ventilation.*"[186]

One of the difficulties I have observed with Management Conversations over the years is what a former colleague of mine described as Random Acts of Safety. Random acts of safety speaks to the

---

[186] Pike River, p. 53.

idea that managers are just going out and generally talking about safety. Managers often engage in Management Conversations without any real understanding of the applicable workplace health and safety management systems or processes, so they often have no idea whether they are confirming the implementation of the requirements of the workplace health and safety management system and the efficacy of those requirements.

It is equally likely that by engaging in a conversation about workplace health and safety with a worker, without an adequate knowledge of the organisation's workplace health and safety requirements, the manager could be reinforcing unsafe work practices, or at least practices that are not consistent with the organisation's requirement. These types of conversations left unchecked and unverified rather than help manage legal risk in the organisation may actually be creating it by contributing to long-term non-compliance with the organisations processes – a concept of systemic failure.

At the same time, Management Conversations often operate under a system of "*criticality by coincidence*".

Without proper planning and structure, the likelihood of a Management Conversation providing meaningful insight into the important elements required to understand if the organisations workplace health and safety processes are operating as intended and are effective to manage workplace health and safety hazards, which seem to be a product of good luck rather than good management.

Unfortunately, my experience of workplace health and safety metrics is that the "*number*" or "*traffic light*" reveals nothing about the critical assumptions underpinning the whole system of Management Conversations

Percentage of corrective actions from incident investigations closed out on time

Another common workplace health and safety metric that appears in monthly workplace health and safety reports is the percentage of corrective actions from incident investigations closed out within the relevant time frame.

It almost seems trite to have to describe the level of assumption and potential organisational corruption that must necessarily threaten to undermine the credibility of closing out action items as a reliable measure of anything, much less a measure that contributes to some overall picture of the state of workplace health and safety or contribute in any way to evidencing an organisation's legal risk management.

Simply accepting that corrective actions have been closed out because a metric indicates they have is an assumption that needs to be verified from time to time. Public inquiries into major accidents often find that action items reported to be finalised were not. But beyond the simple mechanic of whether corrective actions have in fact been closed out, relying on the closeout of action items from incident investigations as providing any sort of insight into the state of workplace health and safety requires several important assumptions, including assumptions about:

- the skills and competence of investigator;
- the quality of the investigation;
- the suitability of the corrective action;
- the quality and the implementation of the corrective actions; and
- the efficacy of the corrective actions to address the issues identified in the investigation – while also assuming the issues identified in the incident investigation are the "*right*" issues.

Incident investigations are also subject to organisational corruption. Like most things done in the name of workplace health and safety, incident investigations are subject to time and resource pressures and when investigations are subject to timeframes, for example that the investigations must be completed within 28 days, inevitably there will be a trade-off between completing the investigation on time and the quality of the investigation.

It also seems likely that, more than any other area of workplace health and safety management, incident investigations are particularly vulnerable to power and politics within an organisation. Based on conversations I have had with health and safety managers it seems a not uncommon experience that personnel who write incident investigations are directed to "*rewrite*" their investigations or to come up with different findings or conclusions based on more senior management perspectives.

If history is any guide – and in my view it is – organisations should be extraordinarily cautious relying uncritically on their incident investigations to provide effective insight and understanding of workplace health and safety risks in the organisation, much less relying on an amalgamated dataset purporting to evidence that corrective actions from those investigations have been closed out.

Time and again, enquiries have demonstrated that the quality of incident investigations conducted by organisations, or the application of incident investigation processes have been deficient. Examples include:

The Deepwater Horizon Disaster

> *BP conducted its own accident investigation of Deepwater Horizon, but once again kept its scope extremely narrow. Professor Najmedin Meshkati of the University of Southern California, Los Angles—a member of the separate National Academy of Engineering committee investigating the oil spill—criticized BP's accident report for neglecting to "address human performance issues and organizational factors which, in any major accident investigation, constitute major contributing factors." He added that BP's investigation also ignored factors such as fatigue, long shifts, and the company's poor safety culture.*[187]

Montara

> *The Inquiry considers that the manner in which PTTEPAA approached Inquiry itself provides further evidence of the company's poor governance. [They] did not seek to properly inform [themselves about] the circumstances and the causes of the Blowout. ... [They] carried out a very cursory and inadequate investigation of the causes of the Blowout.*[188]

BP Texas City

> *BP acknowledges the importance of incident and near miss investigations ... Although BP is improving aspects of its incident and near miss investigation process, BP has not instituted effective ... procedures to identify systemic causal factors that may contribute to future accidents.*[189]

Esso Longford

> *Had the incident on 28 August 1998 been reported as it should have been, the [dangers] would, in all probability, have become known as would the steps available to avert the danger. The failure to report this incident thus stand as another example of a failure in Esso's implementation of its management systems.*[190]

---

[187] Deepwater Report, p. 223.
[188] Montara, p. 12.
[189] Baker Panel Review, p. xiv.
[190] Longford Royal Commission, [13.148].

On Metrics

Given the historical performance of incident investigations as revealed by major accident inquiries, most organisations should be very reluctant to put too much faith in their systems of incident investigations as providing useful support to their systems of workplace health and safety management.

If you want to understand how the quality of incident investigations play out from a legal risk management perspective, consider the following cross examination that arose during the Pike River Royal Commission.[191]

> Q. *That incident accident form, I wonder if I could have it up please, Ms Basher. DAO.001.00359/15.*
>
> **WITNESS REFERRED TO DOCUMENTS DAO.001.00359/15**
>
> Q. *That's the 5th of October incident. It's got that same number in the top corner there, and then 16 please, Ms Basher. That summarises the auxiliary fan blade being sheared off and so on. Do you see that Mr White?*
>
> A. *Yeah.*
>
> Q. *Seventeen, there's the event set out in some detail, /17 please Ms Basher.*
>
> A. *Yep.*
>
> Q. *And then two pages on, /19, just the page in between seems to be a complete blank, "Discussion topics", and I just want to look at the list of improvements, these are matters that had to be worked on as a result of this incident, were they?*
>
> A. *Yes, they were.*
>
> Q. *First one, "Lack of working communication devices underground." What devices are we talking about and what was done to solve that problem?*
>
> A. *I'm not entirely sure what communication devices they're talking about, whether it was phones, DACs or gas monitoring, it doesn't make it clear enough in there to say what actual communication devices they're talking about.*
>
> Q. *Well, you saw this – presumably you saw this accident –*
>
> A. *Yes, I did see this accident report, yeah.*
>
> Q. *And you would've done the sign off on this one?*
>
> A. *I did and sent it on to the Department of Labour.*

---

[191] Pike River Royal Commission, Transcript of phase 3 hearing commencing 13 February 2012 at Greymouth.

Q. *So wouldn't you have inquired into what was not working underground in terms of communication devices?*

A. *I may well have done at the time Mr Hampton, I can't remember.*

Q. *"Lack of communication to the surface fan." What was done to rectify that?*

A. *Again I can't remember what communication they're talking about, whether that would be telemetric or whatever. These recommendations were handled by the electrical engineering department. I can't sit here and confirm which ones were done and which weren't done.*

Q. *Well, as mine manager isn't that your responsibility to find out what was being done and what wasn't being done? Weren't you the man responsible.*

OBJECTION: MR HAIGH (14:27:14) – NOT TO ANSWER

CROSS-EXAMINATION CONTINUES: MR HAMPTON

Q. *Third bullet point, "No set and relevant procedures to follow (starting generators)." Was there no procedures for the starting of generators?*

A. *It would appear from this at that point there wasn't.*

Q. *Was there by the 19th of November?*

A. *I'm – I make the assumption that there was. I'm fairly certain there was in fact.*

Q. *"Could not find fan spares in stock. They were on site but not stocked." 15 Was that rectified?*

A. *Again, I would like to think that was rectified, yeah.*

Q. *"Could not find fan drawings and manuals easily." That was –*

A. *As I've said Mr Hampton, I can't honestly say which ones of these were rectified and not rectified.*

Q. *So just running down them, that's going to be the same answer to all of them, is it?*

A. *Yes.*

Q. *"The IMT early on, the fresh air base with to what's in it, gas monitoring spares and procedures need to be addressed." Can I pause on that one? Was it addressed?*

A. *Again Mr Hampton, I cannot remember, so I cannot say if it was or it wasn't.*

Q. *"Check that monitor station 7 reads methane not carbon monoxide."*

A.   *I would like to think that was done. How many times do I have to say that? I can't sit here and remember whether all these were done or not. Because it wasn't actually, wasn't actually my responsibility to physically get these things done.*

A.   *But surely it's part of your responsibility if you sign off and send it on to Department of Labour, your responsibility to make sure that these things are done, isn't it?*

OBJECTION: MR HAIGH (14:29:14) – NOT TO ANSWER

...

Q.   *Second from the top, 24th August 2010, 1031, "A sparky," sorry, 24th of August you were then statutory mine manager?*

A.   *That was one of my roles, yes.*

Q.   *"A sparky was unbolting the electrical cabinet whilst power was on. I asked him if he should isolate it first before opening the door. He said, 'No. The power should be shut-off once the door opens.' He then opened the door in front of me. I asked another sparky if it should isolated, and he said, 'Yes,' so I told the undermanager. Unsafe act, 10 significant hazard, yes." Did this incident come to your notice?*

A.   *Yes it certainly did.*

Q.   *Has the potential for a gas ignition that sort of event?*

A.   *Absolutely yes.*

Q.   *What was done to remedy it?*

A.   *That particular electrician was, for want of a better word, withdrawn from service and completely retrained. He claimed that he had seen it happen before and his claims were thoroughly investigated and it was established that he hadn't seen it happen before. He was lacking in knowledge in that respect. Like I say, that triggered that particular individual being completely retrained.*

Q.   *Why is that not recorded in the remedial actions?*

A.   *Mr Hampton I didn't do this report, that should have been. That should also have been signed-off that one by the engineering manager.*

Q.   *What was there in place to ensure that these incident/accident forms were being properly investigated, remedied and signed off?*

A.   *It's fair to say that everyone knew what the system was supposed to be as far as investigation and sign-off, but it's obvious from what you're putting in front of me, Mr Hampton, that wasn't done on a number of occasions.*

> *Q.   Does that disturb you?*
>
> *A.   It's concerning.*
>
> *Q.   Was there a degree of dysfunction throughout the whole administration of this mine?*
>
> *A.   I wouldn't say there was a large degree of dysfunction, as I say, there were certain areas that could certainly have been improved.*
>
> *Q.   Particular areas?*
>
> *A.   Not going to be specific on that. Improvements could've been made in a number of areas with respect to, well, here's one for example, how incident reports were dealt with and signed off.*

Percentage of workplace health and safety training completed

I think it is uncontroversial that training and competence is central to effective workplace health and safety management and to an organisation's legal obligations under the Model WHS Act. The primary duty under the Model WHS Act, to ensure so far as is reasonably practicable the health and safety of workers and others, includes a specific obligation to ensure so far as is reasonably practicable:

> *the provision of any information, training, instruction or supervision that is necessary to protect all persons from risks to their health and safety arising from work carried out as part of the conduct of the business or undertaking;[192]*

It is unsurprising that the organisation would want to create and keep records of the workplace health and safety training it provides to its workers and others, and doing so makes perfect sense from both a workplace health and safety and a legal risk management perspective. However, for the reasons we have discussed – assumptions and organisational corruption – relying on a measure like the percentage of workplace health and safety training completed against target is not a helpful metric.

At best, a number or traffic light indicating compliance with a training metric tells us that people have "*done*" the relevant training. But ensuring that training is done is not a guarantee of workplace health and safety, and it does not effectively exercise an organisation's legal obligations. Organisations need to ensure that training is:

- fit for purpose;
- provided;
- understood by the participants;

---

[192]   Model WHS Act section19(3)(f).

- implemented in practice in the workplace; and
- monitored and enforced.

Training and competence is almost always highlighted as a failing in accident investigations and inquiries and we can point to example after example where investigations and inquiries have criticised training and competence. For example, during the Longford Royal Commission, Esso had argued that their operators were well-trained and failed to deal with basic, well understood hazards on the day the incident. The Royal Commission took a different view, finding that the *"real cause"* of the disaster was training:

> *Notwithstanding the matters mentioned above, the conclusion is inevitable that the accident ... would not have occurred had appropriate steps being taken ... Those who were operating [Gas Plant 1] on 25 September 1998 did not have knowledge of the dangers associated with the loss of lean oil flow and did not take the steps necessary to avert those dangers. Nor did those charged with the supervision of the operations have the necessary knowledge and the steps taken by them were inappropriate. The lack of knowledge on the part of both operators and supervisors was directly attributable to a deficiency in their initial or subsequent training. Not only was there training inadequate, but there were no current operating procedures to guide them in dealing with the problems which they encountered on 25 September 1998.[193]*

In the Harris decision[194], a worker was injured when they fell off and ironically named *"safety step"*. The worker's employer tried to rely on its training and induction processes as evidence that he had discharged its obligations for workplace health and safety, but the practical impact of that training did not support the employer's position:

> *The defendant's induction package is lengthy and it covers many matters of employment, courtesy, health and safety issues, and the use of a great deal of equipment. Many of the items initialled by the plaintiff appear irrelevant to her job, although she did recall "Dave" demonstrating to her use of the garbage compactor. She said she had no idea how to use items such as an electric pallet jack, which is one of the items she had initialled. She maintained she had never been shown in her induction or training how to use*

---

193 Longford Royal Commission, p. 234.
194 *Harris v Coles Supermarkets Australia Pty Ltd* [2017] ACTSC 81 (**Harris**).

*the safety step, but had merely followed another employee,
and how that employee had been using the step.[195]*

The number, or percentage of training programs completed reported as an indicator of health and safety performance is simply a measure of activity, it is an indicator of process and not an indicator of the outcomes an organisation needs to understand.

In the Baker Panel review there were observations about the lack of rigour in the training and its inability to actually assess worker knowledge:

> *For example, a 2001 root cause analysis report relating to an incident at the Toledo refinery involving an operator stated that the training system does not fully assess if a person has mastered the material being taught, noting that the operator in question passed a training test with a 100% score.*

> *Although employees must eventually pass the computer-based tests, BP's U.S. refineries commonly provided repeated opportunities for employees to retake the same tests if needed. Some employees suggested that these repeat opportunities were almost unlimited.[196]*

If there is one thing, over and above everything else, which I believe would have a real and lasting impact on health and safety performance, health and safety management and do more than anything else to protect the lives of workers and other people affected by business, it would be a significant, real and meaningful investment in training and competence. If we can only manage to remove bureaucracy from one area of health and safety management, this is where it should be.

DUE DILIGENCE INDEX

If we look at one recent attempt to align workplace health and safety metrics with modern safety thinking, the Due Diligence Index, we can see that the attempt does not take us any further than historic lead safety metrics.

The Due Diligence Index was initially presented as an academic paper but was subsequently reinterpreted to what seems to be an operational model, called the Due Diligence Index Standard.[197] For the

---

[195] Harris, [40].

[196] Baker Panel Review, p. 164.

[197] (2021) (DDI-S) Standard: Standard & Guidance for Use. Due Diligence Index Council (**Due Diligence Standard**).

sake of distinction moving forward, I will refer to the Due Diligence Index paper as the *Due Diligence Paper*, and the Standard as the *Due Diligence Standard*.

Both the Due Diligence Paper and the Due Diligence Standard make significant claims about being a compliance tool for obligations under health and safety legislation. The Due Diligence Paper states:

> *The potentially measurable and certainly demonstrable capacities elaborated below are not only consistent with existing and emerging research in safety and resilience engineering, they also exhaustively cover the due diligence requirements under typical work safety legislation in many Western countries ...*
>
> *...*
>
> *a capacity index that captures the requirements of exercising such reasonable care and diligence would more readily reflect the legal requirements expected of directors and managers of companies and represent a better guide to compliance with such duties.*

The Due Diligence Standard makes claims about its close alignment with WHS Legislation in Australia, including a claim that it is based on the "*high-water mark of the legislative obligations placed on officers to exercise due diligence under health and safety laws in jurisdictions such as Australia and New Zealand*".[198]

In my view, neither the Due Diligence Standard nor the Due Diligence Paper take us any further in demonstrating that our organisations are "*safe*" or evidencing legal compliance.

What the Due Diligence Standard does is propose 6 elements, *Know, Understand, Resource, Monitor, Comply,* and *Verify* which have corresponding activities or measures assigned to them. For example, the element *Know* is measured by "*worker insight experience feedback weighting by the percentage of worker insights effectively closed out per million hours worked*". The *Monitor* element is measured by the "*number of learning reviews and learning teams per million hours worked*".

The measure or activity associated with each element produces a ranking on a scale of 1 to 5, with 1 being the lowest and 5 being the highest, which in turn produces a descriptor associated with each ranking:

---

[198] Due Diligence Standard, p. 6.

Rating	DDI-S Descriptor	Resilience Descriptor
1	Critical	Change Essential
2	Fragile	Deficient
3	Brittle	Rudimentary
4	Resilient	Stable
5	Optimal	Industry Leadership

The *"Due Diligence Index – Safety"* is based on an average of the five elements.[199].

While the Due Diligence Index may have attempted to align itself with the elements of the due diligence obligation described in section 27 of the Model WHS Act, it does not usefully address the legal compliance obligations, and attempts to describe compliance obligations are not consistent with judicial interpretations of due diligence for workplace health and safety in Australia.

While the philosophies underpinning the idea of a Due Diligence Index might align with modern safety thinking, the mechanics of the Due Diligence Standard are no different from the existing metrics, including the examples we have analysed above. Moreover, there is nothing in the numbers produced by the Due Diligence Standard that:

- provide any useful insight – and certainly no more than any other metric –into the state of workplace health and safety;
- demonstrates that an organisation is meeting its obligations under Australian health and safety legislation; or
- demonstrates that officers of a PCBU are meeting their obligations under Australian health and safety legislation.

These issues can be explained by a detailed examination of Element 1 of the Due Diligence Standard, *"Know"*.

The *Know* element of the Due Diligence Standard is described as:

> *"Acquire and keep up-to-date of health and safety matters"[200],*

with this definition seemingly taken directly from section 27(5)(a) of the Model WHS Act.

The number which purports to represent an organisation's ranking against the *"know"* element of the Due Diligence Standard is drawn from

---

[199] Due Diligence Standard, p. 9.
[200] Due Diligence Standard, p. 11.

a process described as *"worker insights"*.[201] Worker insights are described as:

> *Mechanisms, activities and initiatives established in the organisation to generate engagement from and with workers at a site or operational level on health and safety matters with that worker insight being used to inform decision making and health and safety leadership. Organisational leaders (including Board members and Executives) are to be involved in obtaining those worker insights.*[202]

It is worth noting from the outset that this definition of *"worker insights"* is confusing and seems to mean different things at different points in the Due Diligence Standard.

The first part of the definition of *"worker insights"* appears to define them as an activity. That is something that is established in the organisation to generate engagement on workplace health and safety matters between workers and executives.

However, the worker insights also appear to be designed to produce an outcome. Although it is not overtly described in the Due Diligence Standard, it appears that the activity of conducting a worker insight should produce ideas, suggestions or action items. Unhelpfully, these outcomes also appear to be called *"worker insights"*.

The second part of the definition of worker insights says that organisational leaders will be involved in *"obtaining"* those worker insights.

This distinction between the activity and the outcome is never clearly articulated in the Due Diligence Standard.

For the sake of clarity, and when necessary, I will refer to the *"activity"* of a worker insight as the *"worker engagement"* and the *"output"* of a worker insight as the *"workers ideas"*. The importance of the distinction between these two interpretations of what a *"worker insight"* might be will become apparent as we analyse the mechanics of the process.

There are several component parts to the mechanics of the worker insight process, all of which are similar to existing processes that form the basis of current metrics – lead indicators – for measuring workplace health and safety.

---

[201] *Element 1 – Know,* of the Due Diligence Standard is described at pages 11 – 15 of the Due Diligence Standard.

[202] Due Diligence Standard, p. 12.

First, an important measure is the number of worker insights performed weighted by frequency, with the number of worker insights performed generating a score and the greater the number of worker insights performed per million hours worked, the higher the score.[203]

Total number of Worker Insights per 1 million hours worked	Insight Frequency Rate Score (IFRS)
0– 500	1
500 – 1000	2
1000 – 1500	3
1500 – 2000	4
> 2000	5

This is the first example where the question of terminology and the definition of *"worker insight"* become somewhat problematic. When the Due Diligence Standard talks about the *"total number of worker insights"* is it talking about the number of *"worker engagements"* conducted, or the number of *"workers ideas"* generated? There is no logical reason why it could not be either.

In either case, worker engagements or worker ideas, the inputs and outputs are problematic.

There is no explanation in either the Due Diligence Paper or the Due Diligence Standard about how the relative number of worker insights performed are rated. For example, what research supports the idea that conducting between 500 – 1000 worker insights per million hours worked should receive a score of 2, as opposed the idea that conducting between 1500 – 2000 worker insight per million hours worked warrants a score of 4? Why is the later twice as good?

Immediately we can see the similarity to problems with pre-existing lead indicators of safety performance. While the authors of the Due Diligence Standard do attempt to add some qualitative assessment to worker insights, the first obvious issue is that, like most lead indicators of workplace health and safety performance, the *"Insight Frequency Rate Score"* is a measure of activity. There is an inherent presumption that worker insights[204] are a *"good"* thing for safety, and that more of them is *"better"*.

A second obvious issue is the potential for organisational corruption. If part of an organisation needs to increase its rating against the Due Diligence Index, it can:

---

[203] Due Diligence Standard, p.14.
[204] Either conducting work engagements or producing workers ideas.

- do more worker engagements; or
- generate more workers ideas.

However, there is no guarantee that the generation of more activity will necessarily have a benefit for safety – particularly if the activity is being generated to produce a score on a dashboard. This is the classic foundation for creating a disconnect between purpose and process.

It is not difficult to foresee the application of organisational pressure leading to parts of organisations (or even entire organisations) generating worker insights (however defined) to produce a number for a dashboard completely disconnected from the health and safety objectives of the exercise.

It also begs the question is every worker idea generated from a worker engagement something that has to be accepted and implemented?

If the answer that question is *"yes"*, and every worker idea needs to be accepted and implemented, then it is hard to see how the process could be practical. How would an organisation possibly resource and deliver against that volume of workplace health and safety initiatives? How could the organisation assure that worker ideas generated in one worker engagement did not contradict or undermine worker ideas generated in another worker engagement? And in light of my earlier comments in relation to wicked problems that solutions to workplace health and safety problems often generate other problems in the longer term, how will the organisation monitor the long-term effect of this multitude of worker ideas?

If the answer to the question is *"no"*, and there will be a selection or filtering process of worker ideas generated via worker engagements, how will the organisation assure the integrity of that filtering process?

If the criteria that the organisation or parts of it are being assessed against is the number of worker ideas closed out, then it is not unforeseeable that part of the organisation will manipulate their worker engagements to produce smaller numbers of easily closed out worker ideas. Other difficulties around any *"selection"* process for worker ideas include:

- potentially disengaging workers from the process – in much the same way that hazard reporting and incident investigations have been shown to disengage workers when they do not see any outcomes from the process; or
- having to establish reporting mechanisms to report back to participants in work engagements which of their ideas will be

implemented, and potential follow-up and communication around those ideas.

None of this is to say that creating engagements between all levels of organisations to discuss workplace health and safety and to allow operational personnel to provide feedback on the efficacy of safety management, and for management personnel to understand the suitability of their workplace health and safety initiatives is not a good idea. However, once you burden that conversation with a process, particularly a process that contains scoring mechanisms designed to produce a report to go to senior management, organisations need to think very long and very hard about:

- their capacity to properly resource that process;
- the assumptions underpinning the process; and
- the potential for the process to be corrupted to produce "*green*" indicators which may not be a true reflection of what process was designed to achieve.

Another important measure described in the Due Diligence Standard which contributes to the "*know*" score is the percentage of worker insights effectively closed out.[205]

This is another example where the question of terminology and the definition of "*worker insight*" is problematic. When the Due Diligence Standard talks about the effective closeout of a worker insight, is it talking about the effect of closeout of a "*worker engagement*", or of the "*workers ideas*"? And as discussed above, if worker ideas, which ones?

If the Due Diligence Standard is interested in effectively closing out worker engagements, this would seem a wholly mechanistic and pointless activity. It is akin to counting the number of management meetings held each month to determine the effectiveness of an organisation's management.

If the Due Diligence Standard is interested in effectively closing out workers ideas (which offers at least some potential benefit), then it is subject to the same types of issues we discussed earlier when it comes to the closeout of any other type of action items, for example those derived from incident investigations.

Relying on the percentage of workers ideas closed out carries with it a range of assumptions about things like:

- the quality of those ideas;

---

[205] Due Diligence Standard, p. 13.

- the relevance of those ideas to the organisation's workplace health and safety risks;
- whether the ideas have been closed out *"in fact"* or simply on paper;
- whether the ideas have been effectively implemented; or
- whether the ideas positively contribute to workplace health and safety, or, potentially, make things worse.

So far, structurally, there is nothing inherent in the worker insight process that makes it any more beneficial as a leading indicator of workplace health and safety performance then any number of other indicators. And structurally, it has characteristics that have been shown to compromise the integrity of these types of metrics, including:

- aligning a score to the number of activities performed, with higher scores given to more activity; and
- measuring the percentage of action items completed.

The authors of the Due Diligence Standard have added an additional layer of process to the worker insights mechanic in what appears to be an attempt to provide a qualitative assessment of the process. This is described as a *"worker insight experience evaluation feedback"*.[206]

The worker insight experience process is described as an *"assessment of the experience of the worker insight activity or initiative"* (what I would understand to be the worker engagement). The process involves each worker and leader who participated in the worker insight (i.e., the worker engagement not each individual workers idea) to rank their experience:

- In the case of workers: on a scale of 1 – 5, with 5 being the highest, *"was I heard during that experience?"*
- In the case of a leader: on a scale of 1 – 5, with 5 being the highest, *"did I gain valuable insight through that experience?"*

Not only does the worker insight experience evaluation feedback add another layer of process to the exercise, staff feedback and surveys have their own issues as a reliable measure and have their own set of assumptions and potential organisational corruption, such as bias with self-reported data in surveys or feeling pressured, to report positively. The pressure to report positively may be particularly prevalent when the

---

[206] Due Diligence Standard, p. 12.

survey contributes to something like accreditation, or in the case of the Due Diligence Standard, a metric of safety performance.[207]

While I can understand the reason behind trying to understand people's perspective of their involvement in a worker engagement, using a survey score to feed into a metric creates additional layers of assumption and potential organisational corruption that needs verification and assurance.

Just the analysis of this one element of the Due Diligence Standard raises an issue about how many organisations would actually have the time and resources to properly implement and assess this type of workplace health and safety initiative?

Having gone through the process (presumably multiple processes) of worker insights we arrive at a score, which places the organisation somewhere between *"critical"* and *"optimal"* against the *"know"* measure of the Due Diligence Index.

What is clear, however, is that the quality of any ideas generated by the worker insight process or the contribution the ideas might make to workplace health and safety ***is not measured and does not contribute to the score***.

Putting a metric like worker insights into the context of the historical application of lead indicators for workplace health and safety performance, it seems clear that it is susceptible to all the assumptions and organisational corruption that has gone before, and there are multiple points of assurance and verification which need to be considered just to have confidence that the measure is even being performed well.

Again, with history as a guide, it is entirely foreseeable that parts of an organisation could achieve optimal (*"industry leadership"*[208]) performance against the *"know"* criteria with nothing more than a bureaucratic manipulation of the volume of activity and with no worthwhile contribution to workplace health and safety.

The authors of the Due Diligence Standard seem to recognise this possibility, but account for it in a very curious way. At page 15, the Due Diligence Standard says:

> *[The worker insights] measure requires organisations to*
> *monitor what insights are being provided by workers in*
> *terms of suggestions for approaches to health and safety*
> *management in practice and then monitor the extent to*

---

[207] Hogden, A., Ellis, L, Churruca, K and M. Bierbaum. (2017). Safety Culture Assessment in Health Care: A review of the literature on safety culture assessment tools. Australian Institute of Health Innovation | Macquarie University, pp. 20 – 21.

[208] Due Diligence Standard, p. 9.

which those insights are actually being implemented in practice. It is not sufficient to merely rely upon whether the suggested actions have been implemented. Assessments of the effectiveness of close-out of worker insights must also include consideration of whether those worker insights are leading to better health and safety performance in the organisation and having a positive impact on the organisation and its health and safety capacity.

However, there is no accounting or weighting for that qualitative assessment - the qualitative assessment is not accounted for on the formula and does not contribute to the assessment of the organisation's achievement against the *"know"* criteria of the Due Diligence Standard. This appears to mean that an organisation could have a raft of worker insights that do not lead to better health and safety performance in the organisation and are not having a positive impact on the organisation and its health and safety capacity, but nevertheless could still have a really good score against the *"know"* criteria.

It would seem that fundamentally the measure of workplace health and safety performance proposed by the worker insight metric is nothing more than a measure of activity similar, if not identical, to existing lead indicators and susceptible to exactly the same assumptions and organisational corruption.

The only qualification to this is that in the case of worker insights, the process adds a further layer of administration in the form of the worker insight experience evaluation feedback – a separate layer of process complete with its own assumptions and potential for organisational corruption.

The authors of the Due Diligence Standard also provide further interesting commentary by way of *"Reporting Guidance"*. On page 15 of the Due Diligence Standard it says:

organisations are encouraged to provide reporting commentary with respect to the processes for how they are assessing the effectiveness of close out on worker insights. That is, how is the organisation and its leadership assuring themselves that the solutions identified by workers for better health and safety performance through work insights are being implemented and are effective and fit for purpose.

Having gone through what seems to be an overly complicated engagement and feedback process to obtain a dashboard score which management (unsurprisingly) might assume is designed to tell them something about the state of workplace health and safety, "*someone*" still has to provide information about:

- the extent to which insights are "*actually being implemented in practice*";
- whether worker insights are leading to better health and safety performance in the organisation and having a positive impact on the organisation and its health and safety capacity; and
- how the organisation and the leadership are assuring themselves that the solutions identified by workers for better health and safety performance through work insights are being implemented and are effective and fit for purpose.

This seems to be a very curious, but to my mind, unsurprising position to arrive at. Once again it reinforces the importance of the narrative over the number - we need to engage in a conversation with executive management to provide a qualitative descriptor of our assessment of workplace health and safety management in our organisation rather than provide them with numbers and graphs.

The fact that the Due Diligence Standard still requires a narrative exercise about the state of workplace health and safety management in the organisation does seem to make the whole administrative exercise of producing a number, to go on a pressure gauge, to display on a dashboard, somewhat pointless.

If my workplace health and safety "*numbers*" cannot tell me if my safety initiatives:

- have been implemented in practice;
- are leading to better health and safety performance and having a positive impact on health and safety; and
- the health and safety solutions of the organisation are implemented, effective and fit for purpose,

why bother having the number?

Noting that none of these factors, which seem far more important than any of the factors that actually make up the "*know*" score actually contribute to that score.

Indeed, these observations in the Due Diligence Standard go directly to the problems of health and safety metrics as they currently stand, including the problems inherent in the Due Diligence Standard.

Health and safety metrics cannot tell us whether the processes we have designed to manage the health and safety hazards and risks in our business are:

- fit for purpose;

- well implemented; and
- effective to manage the workplace health and safety hazards and risks.

If we could do these things – if we could identify and evidence these factors – we would not need a Due Diligence Index. But to create a complicated administrative process and then *have to provide the narrative assessment anyway* seems somewhat pointless.

Just provide the narrative.

That is not to dismiss the importance of engagement at all levels of the organisation, and by all levels of the organisation with each other, about workplace health and safety. Having conversations and engagements with workers very likely will provide valuable insights into whether our systems to manage workplace health and safety hazards and risks are fit for purpose, implemented, and effective – but to overlay conversations with administrative processes and convoluted calculations to produce a number for a dashboard which does not address any of the real issues we need to understand is not helpful. Further, as already discussed, it is more likely than not to simply contribute to the ongoing illusion of safety created by traditional measures of safety.

VERIFYING METRICS

One of the inherent characteristics of reasonably practicable (and hence individual due diligence) is to understand if the organisation has proper systems to manage the workplace health and safety risks in the business and adequate assurance to know if those systems are in place and effective. Further, it is inherent in the notion of due diligence that those required to exercise due diligence bring an independent mind and critical thought to the relevant subject matter.

The way that health and safety information is usually presented, with an almost exclusive reliance on charts, graphs, and data – including traffic light scores against lead indicators, makes it almost impossible for the organisation to demonstrate compliance with its legal obligations, or for individuals to demonstrate they have exercised due diligence.

An inherent problem with most workplace health and safety metrics is that it is very difficult – it is possible at all – to verify the contents of the metrics, or to analyse the data that goes to make up the metrics.

We can compare this to something like financial metrics. When a company board looks at the organisation's financial metrics, it can look at the headline data – for example profit, but also review the information that goes into making up that profit number. Further, both the profit number and the underlying contributors to that number can be checked, verified, and audited. And verification is a critical element of due diligence.

This verification process is not so easy for workplace health and safety metrics.

If I receive a monthly metric telling me how many management conversations have been held, it is very difficult to deconstruct that number to understand what it means. What were the management conversations about? What did we learn in the conversations? Did the management conversations deal with critical safety processes or risks, or were they focussed on lower lever issues like the use of personal protective equipment? Did the management conversation give us any insight into whether our workplace health and safety processes are fit for purpose, implemented and effective?

It is entirely possible that a board could receive a monthly health and safety report with a *"green"* traffic light against the requirements for management conversations, without having any insight at all into the state of health and safety management in the organisation.

As an aside, I would note that financial metrics also provide some information directly relevant to issues the board want to understand. If the board want to know the profitability of the business, monthly profitability data provides that information.

If a board want to know if the business is managing its obligations for workplace health and safety, the number of management conversations held in the business over a 6-month period does not answer that question. Nor do any other current metrics. At their highest, some metrics may indicate the completion of an activity which, if done well, may make some contribution to safety.

TIME FOR A NEW APPROACH TO ASSURANCE?

It is difficult, in my view, to make an argument that an organisation can have any confidence in the state of safety management based on traditional workplace health and safety metrics because those metrics do not proactively demonstrate or evidence whether there are proper systems to manage the hazards in the business and that those systems are implemented and effective. Indeed, as we saw from the earlier discussions around *"worker insights"* in the Due Diligence Standard, those elements (proper systems and assurance) are not present in the indicator of *"know"*. The Due Diligence Standards requires a further narrative add-on to the metric (which does not contribute to the score) to explain how the organisation knows it has proper systems to manage the hazards and that those systems are implemented and effective.

A 'numbers' or metrics-based approach simply does not give organisations or their leaders insights into the efficacy of workplace health and safety management, and can hide critical safety issues.

For example, if an organisation's management was trying to understand if confined space risks in the organisation were being well managed (proper systems and adequate supervision), there is nothing inherent in traditional metrics (or anything proposed by methodologies such as the Due Diligence Standard) that would bring this to their attention. Further, as illustrated above it would be extraordinarily difficult to "*unpick*" the "*green traffic light*" (or "*pressure gauge*" in the case of the Due Diligence Standard) to isolate the information that forms part of that indicator to a specific risk like confined space entry.

So, what might a different framework look like?

I think the starting point is to move away from the idea of trying to report workplace health and safety as a number and embrace the story of workplace health and safety as a narrative.

PART 7
A FRAMEWORK FOR PROVING SAFETY

The best minds in the senior leadership of a company should be paying close attention to those risks. But it didn't happen here. And now we are all paying the consequences because those of you at the top don't seem to have a clue about what was going on on this rig.[209]

---

[209] *The role of BP in the Deepwater Horizon explosion and oil spill*, Thursday, June 17, 2010. House of Representatives, Subcommittee on Oversight and Investigations, Committee on Energy and Commerce, Washington, D.C., Page 129 – 130

Given the themes explored in this book, and the case history surrounding workplace health and safety, I think it is evident that we need a different way to think about and understated the efficacy of our processes for managing workplace health and safety.

Many organisations invest significantly in workplace health and safety management, which includes a significant expenditure in time and money dedicated to the collection and management of workplace health and safety data and the collation of workplace health and safety metrics. But what is the output of this expenditure?

From a legal risk management perspective, our efforts to produce data and metrics evidencing the efficacy of our workplace health and safety management do not amount to anything of value. Universally, there is nothing in a typical workplace health and safety report that can be used by a defendant in a prosecution under health and safety legislation to demonstrate that an organisation was meeting its legal obligations. There is nothing in a typical workplace health and safety report that answers the fundamental, foundational questions:

- Do we have proper systems to manage the workplace health and safety risks in our business?
- What level of assurance do we have that the systems we do have are implemented and effective to manage the workplace health and safety risks?

And if our processes for reporting on health and safety outcomes cannot answer basic, legal risk management questions, what can they tell us about the state of health and safety in our organisation? Again, with history as our guide, apparently very little, if anything.

So, what might a different framework look like?

I think the starting point is to move away from the idea of trying to report workplace health and safety as a number and embrace the story of workplace health and safety as a narrative.

Workplace health and safety reporting should be a narrative report describing:

- what assurance activities were undertaken during the relevant reporting period;
- what those assurance activities revealed about the state of the organisation's systems to manage health and safety; and
- whether those systems were implemented and effective.

This idea of workplace health and safety reporting as a narrative is not an exercise in *"command and control"* safety, or *"Traditional"* safety.

It need not be a surveillance exercise designed to achieve compliance with "*work as imagined*".

Regardless of how an organisation "*does*" workplace health and safety, workplace health and safety management is founded on certain organisational beliefs, principles, or expectations – even if those beliefs, principles, or beliefs are not given voice or publicly stated.

If workplace health and safety is founded on principles of local adaptability where workers are free to "*vary locally*" to meet the changing demands of their day-to-day work, then that system creates certain expectations. And those expectations can be tested. It should be possible to be in a workplace and observe whether the organisations expectations for workplace health and safety management are being met.

Our current systems of workplace health and safety reporting do not give us any helpful insight into our expectations.

If workplace health and safety management in an organisation is founded on command and control and procedural compliance, the number of management conversations completed or the number of investigation corrective actions closed out, do not give us any insight into whether that approach to workplace health and safety management is creating a safer workplace or the "*proper systems/adequate supervision*" question.

In the same way, if workplace health and safety management in an organisation is founded on human and organisational performance principles, the number of management conversations completed or the number of investigation corrective actions closed out do not give us any insight into whether that approach to workplace health and safety management is creating a safer workplace or the "*proper systems/adequate supervision*" question.

A system of narrative reporting is a deliberate exercise in reviewing our workplace health and safety process against our expectations. It moves workplace health and safety reporting from a metric collation exercise to a permanent research project.

Narrative workplace health and safety reporting should be founded in specific principles, based on recurring themes that perpetuate through case after case, inquiry after inquiry. Those themes (or questions) are:

- Do we have proper systems to manage the workplace health and safety risks in our business?[210]

---

[210] See for example Hetherington, [40].

- What level of assurance do we have that the systems we do have are implemented and effective to manage the workplace health and safety risks?[211]
- How do we prove the effectiveness of our crucial systems?[212]
- Are fundamental safety procedures in place and effective?[213]
- Are departures form our workplace health and safety expectations *"one-off departures"* from those expectations, or do they represent systemic failures?[214]
- What are the assumptions that underpin the management of workplace health and safety management? Have we surfaced and tested those assumptions?[215]
- Do the workers understand out expectations/processes, and are our systems of workplace health and safety management relevant to their daily activities?[216]

It is my belief that these themes are constant and need to be considered by every organisation in order to understand the efficacy of workplace health and safety management. It is certainly my view that these themes are critical to legal risk management and an organisation's understanding of whether it is meeting its legal obligations under health and safety legislation, but for reasons I have already touched on, I think these themes are also foundational to assuring the safety of workplaces.

Regardless of how an organisation chooses to do workplace health and safety assurance, even if it continues to rely on traditional lead and lag indicators and metrics, I believe that organisations should still overlay the workplace health and safety information they collect with the themes described above.

To better understand workplace health and safety, I think there are several aspects of workplace health and safety management that organisations need to consider to maximise assurance activities.

---

[211] See for example Wollongong Glass, [32].

[212] Pike River, p. 53.

[213] The Ritchie decision, [159].

[214] Wollongong Glass, [32]; the Ritchie decision, [159].

[215] Pike River, p. 18; Piper Alpha, [14.28]; the Ritchie decision, [157].

[216] Queensland Coroner Inquest into the death of Cameron Brandt Cole, p. 22. In this inquest the coroner observed that "*The identification, elimination or minimisation of risks through risk management processes may lead to the production of a suite of documentation that will pass audit requirements. However, the evidence at this inquest suggests that workers in the field may find such documents hard to comprehend and of limited relevance to their daily activities.*"

INTENT

I referred earlier in the book to the notion of *"random acts of safety"*. In proposing a different framework to review and assure workplace health and safety management systems I am proposing a framework built on a common understanding and intent. By this, I mean that the activities we undertake in the name of workplace health and safety should assist us to understand, or be conducted with the purpose of understanding, whether our workplace health and safety management systems are fit for purpose, implemented and effective.

A management conversation is not just a general chat about how things are going, or an opportunity for workers to tell managers what they do not like. Management conversations should be approached with a specific purpose to understand something specific about workplace health and safety management, whether that is to test a worker's understanding of workplace health and safety requirements, or to confirm the rollout of workplace health and safety initiative, or to confirm the efficacy of a corrective action implemented in the workplace. Or to confirm that safety initiatives are meeting to organisation's expectations – regardless, it should have purpose and intent. That is not to say more social aspects of conversations cannot occur,[217] nor is it to say that giving workers the opportunity to raise their grievances is not a very important part of that conversation, but the conversation needs intent.

Similarly, incident investigations should have specific intent.

I think one of the simplest things organisations can do to significantly improve their understanding of workplace health and safety management and bolster legal risk management is to include two straightforward questions as part of every incident investigation or organisational *"deep dive"* into aspects of health and safety management. For the thing being investigated:

- are our systems designed to manage workplace health and safety *"proper systems"*, in so far as they comply with the obligations of legislation, codes of practice and so on; and
- whether, or to what extent, those systems are implemented and effective to manage workplace health and safety.

In the same way, health and safety reporting should have as its foundational purpose, the objective of informing the organisation about

---

[217] It should most definitely not be an exercise in form filling or box ticking conducted behind clipboard.

whether safety management systems are fit for purpose, implemented and effective.

Properly done, I believe that a system of narrative report, narrative description of workplace health and safety management, will allow organisations to create the information necessary to, in the words of the Pike River Royal Commission, prove the effectiveness of the crucial systems.

SAFETY LITERACY

The concepts of workplace health and safety due diligence (both individual and organisational) are not dissimilar from obligations for financial due diligence, and some of the underlying principles of financial literacy. I think a useful starting point to move workplace health and safety assurance forwards is to adopt the idea of *"financial literacy"* to the framework of workplace health and safety.

Financial literacy is a core component of executive management. For example, I have sat on boards and as part of doing that I attended a *"how to read a financial report"* training program, because it was not something that I had ever trained for or was proficient in. However, there does not appear to be any consideration given to a similar level of safety literacy.

Guidance offered by the Australian Securities & Iinvestments Commission on directors and financial reporting[218] makes the following observations:

> *You must take reasonable steps to comply with, or secure compliance with, the financial and audit requirements of the Corporations Act...*
>
> *Each director has a duty of skill, competence and diligence in the understanding of the financial report that is to be disclosed to the public,*
>
> *You must apply your own mind to, and carry out a careful review of, the financial and directors report, determine that the information they contain is consistent with your knowledge of the company's financial position and affairs, and ensure the material matters known to you – or that should be known to you – are not omitted.*

---

[218] https://asic.gov.au/regulatory-resources/financial-reporting-and-audit/directors-and-financial-reporting/#:~:text=INFO%2076)-,Your%20financial%20reporting%20obligations,and%20when%20they%20become%20due

You are entitled to delegate to others the preparation of books and financial reports. However, you are expected to take a diligent and intelligent interest in the information available to you, to understand that information, and apply an inquiring mind.

You must have an appropriate level of financial knowledge, understand your company's business and how it is reflected in the financial report, and apply your knowledge of transactions and events to the financial report.

So, imagine if similar principles were adopted and effectively applied at an executive level of an organisation to workplace health and safety matters. Would the organisation's understanding of workplace health and safety matters, and the delivery of effective health and safety outcomes at work be improved by executive managers who:

- exercised a duty of skill competence and diligence to understand workplace health and safety information;
- applied their own mind and carried out a careful review of workplace health and safety reports; and
- took a diligent and intelligent interest in the workplace health and safety information available to them and applied an "*inquiring mind*" to that information.

I cannot help but think the application of financial literacy principles to safety would significantly improve workplace health and safety outcomes and legal risk. Indeed, I think it is critically important that the health and safety industry works hard to help build workplace health and safety literacy at all levels of organisations.

I remember doing work with a board of a mining company when the Model WHS Act was first adopted in Western Australia, and the board was seeking information about their positive obligations of due diligence. During a break in the board meeting several of the board members were having a discussion about an underground mine fatality in Botswana which involved deaths of two workers. The fatalities occurred during re-entry into the mine after blasting.

Before the board meeting recommenced, I had a discussion with some of the board members to say that the discussion about the Botswana incident was the perfect opportunity for the board to exercise due diligence. The relevant exercise of due diligence works something like this:

- the Botswana incident involved a fatality in an underground mine during re-entry after blasting;

- the board I was working with was a board of an underground mining company in Western Australia;
- one of the workplace health and safety risks at the mine was re-entry after blasting;
- the board should have recognised that re-entry to the mine after blasting was one of workplace health and safety risks in their operation;
- on becoming aware of Botswana incident, the board could proactively ask the chief executive officer to prepare a report or a presentation for the board, at the next board meeting, which explained to the board what the re-entry procedures were for the mine, provide confirmation to the board that the re-entry procedures were "*proper*" procedures that compliant with the requirements of the legislation, codes of practice and so on, and provide evidence to the board about how the company had assurance that the re-entry procedures were implemented and effective.

This type of conversation and approach is entirely consistent with an officer's positive due diligence obligations, and represents, in my view, the type of safety literacy we want to engender in all levels of management in our organisations.

DO LESS, BUT BETTER

For some inexplicable reason it seems to be ingrained in workplace health and safety that doing more of something is qualitatively better than doing less. We saw this earlier in the discussion about the Due Diligence Standard where, for example doing more than 2000 worker insights per 1 million hours worked is more than twice as good as doing between 500 and 1000.[219] Similarly, doing more than 2000 learning team hours per 1 million hours worked is better than doing between 1000 and 1500.[220]

It seems to me that no matter how many worker insights or learning teams you are doing (or management conversations, or incident investigations, or pre-start meetings, or any other safety activities) if they are not achieving the outcome they are designed to achieve, and they are not giving you useful insight into the efficacy of workplace health and safety management, then the practical effect of all these activities is the same as doing nothing at all – and possibly worse than doing nothing.

---

[219] Due Diligence Standard, p. 14.
[220] Due Diligence Standard, p. 18.

I think there is a compelling case in workplace health and safety to do far less workplace health and safety management and make what we do targeted and useful.

For example, is there any real benefit to compelling managers to engage in a certain number of safety conversations a month and count and report against that number? I would think not.

I think there is tremendous benefit in managers spending time at all different levels of the organisation and engaging in conversations on any number of topics which may lead to a greater understanding of issues across the organisation (including workplace health and safety issues), but I am yet to be convinced that this is an exercise which gives the organisation any meaningful insight into the efficacy of workplace health and safety management.

Might there not be more benefit in allowing managers to engage with the organisation when and how they see fit, but holding managers to account to deliver less frequent, but more meaningful and targeted, deep dive analysis of critical health and safety issues within their area of responsibility?

My experience suggests that there is very little accountability for managers with respect to the quality of safety conversations they have with the workforce, sharing lessons from those conversations, or indeed making any sort of contribution to the overall organisational knowledge about workplace health and safety management in the organisation. The only accountability appears to be the number of conversations they engage in.

What if, rather than engaging in a lot of formal, form checking safety conversations, managers were required to conduct a quarterly deep dive into a single critical risk or crucial system relevant to workplace health and safety within their area of responsibility and provide a presentation on that issue to management teams? Or additionally, what if their report on the quarterly deep dive formed an annexure to the health and safety report provided to the board?

It seems to me that this exercise in investigation and narrative reporting will provide the organisation and board far greater insight into the workplace health and safety management systems of the organisation and their efficacy than a green traffic light indicating that everybody has held the requisite number of safety conversations for the month.

Similarly, could we improve workplace health and safety by taking a more targeted approach to front-line risk assessment and work planning? Presently, across many organisations the system of front-line risk assessment and work planning is multilayered and time-consuming, often consisting of:

- a whole group pre-start meeting;
- individual work team planning or pre-start meetings;
- reviewing safe work method statements;
- reviewing job hazard analysis or similar tools; and
- completing an individual risk assessment tool like a Take 5.

Again, in my experience these multiple layers of front-line risk assessment and work planning often duplicate each other, repeat requirements, and it is not uncommon for there to be contradictory requirements between the different layers of documents. Certainly, in my experience this process of front-line risk assessment and work planning is not *"risk"* based. Workers are required to jump through the same hoops and produce the same information regardless of the level of risk.

Research suggests that workers are quite good at undertaking their own risk and work planning quite independently of any mandated or documented requirements.[221] So, if workers are capable of undertaking their own risk and work planning independently of documented processes, perhaps we should allow them to do that.

I think it is worth observing that if workers are not capable of understanding their own risk and work planning independently of documented processes, the document processes are unlikely to help, and it is incumbent on the organisation to:

- understand the competence and capability of their workers; and
- provide training and support to ensure they are competent.

There does seem to me to be an arguable case to allow workers more freedom in risk and work planning, and only impose more rigid standards if we are dealing with high hazard activities, critical risks, or crucial systems/processes.

If workers are engaged in routine work that does not involve high hazard activities, critical risks or crucial systems and processes, do we really need to impose a rigid system of multitiered overlapping front-line risk assessment and work planning? Could our understanding of work health and safety management in our organisation be improved by doing less front-line risk assessment and work planning for low-risk activities

---

[221] See for example *Do take 5 risk assessments contribute to safe work*, Safety of Work Podcast, https://safetyofwork.com/episodes/ep95-do-take-5-risk-assessments-contribute-to-safe-work; Havinga, J.; Shire, M.I.; Rae, A. Should We Cut the Cards? Assessing the Influence of "Take 5" Pre-Task Risk Assessments on Safety. *Safety* 2022, 8, 27. https://doi.org/10.3390/safety8020027.

but investing significantly in planning and risk assessment time and resources when it matters?

Another area where I think *"less but better"* would have a real benefit in understanding workplace health and safety management is incident investigations. The prevalent view in most industries is that all incidents need to be investigated, and the higher the actual or potential severity, the more resources that need to be thrown in the investigation.

As I have already argued, the quality of incident investigations is, in my view, a critical weakness in work health and safety management both from a pure safety perspective and from a legal risk management perspective. I cannot help but think there would be genuine benefits to an organisation that investigated less but investigated better.

I think there are many different ways to achieve greater learnings from incidents than our current methodologies.

For example, would there be benefits to investigating by *"themes"* rather than incidents?

Under this sort of model initial responses to incidents would be a data collection exercise. The data collection process would be designed to understand the basic components of an incident and place that incident in the context of crucial or critical workplace health and safety management issues, as defined by the organisation. This collection of data can be analysed and reviewed to identify recurrent themes or issues, and the organisation can then invest significant time and resources to deep dive, review and really understand those themes and issues.

As an example, it is not uncommon for an incident investigation to identify problems with things such as:

- compliance with procedures;
- failure to identify risk;
- compliance with requirements from training; or
- supervision.

Typically, an incident investigation will deal with those matters in the context of incident and not consider it any further. For example, if the investigation identifies a problem with supervision, you never see any examination of whether the problem of supervision was limited to this particular incident, or whether it represents a systemic failure (or potential systemic failure) in relation to this broader, crucial system of supervision.

Similarly, were an investigation finds that there has been non-compliance with training requirements, almost inevitably the response is to retrain person. Investigation never explores the critical safety and legal risk management questions around things like:

- was this a one-off departure from our training requirements or might be indicative of systemic failure; or
- was the training fit for purpose in the first place; or
- was the person who delivered the training, trained and competent to do so; or
- was the person who developed the training, trained and competent to do so; or
- is the problem with the training identified in this incident limited to this specific training, or is there a broader problem with training delivery and comprehension across the organisation?

If we do baseline data collection on incidents and analyse incidents for themes around crucial systems such as training, supervision and so on, it gives the organisation an opportunity to say, rather than just investigate the incident, we are going to do a deep dive into this crucial system and try and understand across our organisation.

In all three examples described above, management conversations, front-line risk assessment and work planning, and incident investigations, if we move to a "*less but better*" approach we can direct our enquiries in each of those areas to the critical risks and crucial processes that are fundamental to effective workplace health and safety management in the organisation and use each of those activities as a meaningful opportunity to understand:

- if our systems to manage workplace health and safety in our organisation fit and proper; and
- whether, or the extent to which, those systems are implemented and effective.

CRITICALITY

We have observed several times earlier in this book the importance that courts and tribunals place on criticality. In the Pike River Royal Commission, the Royal Commission emphasised the importance of "*crucial systems*"[222] and similarly in the Ritchie decision, the court highlighted "*fundamental safety procedures*".[223]

One of the frustrations that many people have with workplace health and safety is its seeming obsession with trivial aspects of workplace

---

[222] Pike River, p. 53.]
[223] Ritchie, [159].]

health and safety. An example of this is the evolution of safe work method statements over time in Australia.

Safe work method statements are required under health and safety regulations, but they are only required for specific, identified *"high risk construction activities"*. High risk construction activities[224] include work that:

- involves a risk of a person falling more than 2m; or
- involves, or is likely to involve, the disturbance of asbestos; or
- involves structural alterations or repairs that require temporary support to prevent collapse; or
- is carried out in or near a confined space; or
- is carried out in or near a shaft or trench with an excavated depths greater than 1.5 m.

In Western Australia, the regulations stipulate 18 high risk construction activities that require a safe work method statement.

Under health and safety regulations, the safe work method statement must:

- identify the work that is high risk construction work;
- specify hazard relating to the high risk construction work and the risks to health and safety associated with those hazards;
- describe the measures to be implemented to control the risks; and
- describe how the control measures are to be implemented monitored and reviewed.

As a general rule, in my experience, the documents produced as safe work method statements are typically a shambolic mess, being multiple pages long (15+ in many cases) with incoherent risk assessments built off the back of equally incoherent risk matrices. However, they also fail to properly address issues of criticality.

Keeping with the *"more is better"* attitude of the workplace health and safety industry, rather than limit safe work method statements to high risk construction activities, we seem to have taken the view that if a safe work method statement is good for a high risk construction activity, then it must be good for everything, and consequently in many workplaces now we see safe work method statements being used to manage every work-related activity. Unfortunately, when introducing safe work

---

[224] See for example *Work Health and Safety (General) Regulations 2022* (WA), regulation 291.

method statements most organisations did not take it as an opportunity to remove some other process. Rather than use a safe work method statement as the primary tool for managing work, safe work method statements have been slotted into the long list of tools used to manage an activity, including:

- standards;
- procedures;
- toolbox talks;
- pre-start meetings;
- job hazard analysis; and
- Take 5 or similar, differently named personal risk assessments.

Moreover, even when a safe work method statement involves a high-risk work activity, the management of the high-risk work activity is lost in the dross of the overall safe work method statement which almost inevitably includes controls for every single possible activity that could conceivably be associated with the high risk work activity, including slips trips and falls and other minor risks.

What makes the use of safe work method statements in this context so problematic in my view is that they become entirely irrelevant to the workers and importantly dilute the "*high-risk*" message.

If we only used safe work method statements for high-risk work activities, and within the safe work method statement we only focused on the high-risk work activity and the controls critical to the management of that activity, then I think we would be far better positioned to engage workers in the activity and involve them in a process that would be seen as important and relevant. Unfortunately, safe work method statements have become a lost opportunity, simply sliding in to an already crowded space of workplace health and safety administration and bureaucracy.

During one of the multitude of hearings into the Deepwater Horizon disaster there was an exchange of evidence concerning the use of knives on the facility.[225] The evidence is striking insofar as it speaks to the tendency of the health and safety industry to focus on the trivial (often in the name of achieving good metrics) at the expense of understanding the critical risks in the organisation.

---

[225] Testimony of Steve Tink, the health, safety and environmental manager of BP, on 26 May 2010 at the Deepwater Horizon joint investigation hearing as part of the Coast Guard and Minerals Management Service joint investigation launched to determine the cause of the initial incident and fire aboard the mobile offshore drilling unit Deepwater Horizon. (https://www.dvidshub.net/video/316340/1-joint-investigation-hearings-steve-tink)

> *Q.   Could you tell us a little bit about BP's safety policy with respect to the carriage of knives or cutting instruments if you will.*
>
> *Tink.   Basically we only allow people to have approved cutting devices on the rig. So pocket knives or that sort of thing because there has been over time a rash of actual hand injuries where people are using pocket knives. We get cuts – we get reportable injuries so we have approved retractable ... self retracting blades – we use one of the exacto knives with self retracting blades. So there are certain things we do not allow on our facilities so they have to be an approved cutting device.*
>
> *Q.   One of the issues that has arisen through previous testimony is that as the crew were trying to prepare to abandon the vessel an issue came up concerning a tethered life raft to the vessel and the ability to basically sever that tether and get away. There was a lot of focus on the lack of available cutting devices and/or knives. Does your policy apply also to the carriage of equipment inside of lifeboats or life rafts?*
>
> *Tink.   I can't address that. I apologise. I don't, don't know that. I do know that in the day-to-day operations of the facility when people are in the sack room cutting sacks we have approved devices. When it comes to the emergency response I don't have a clear answer for you Sir, I apologise.*

This apparent trade-off between the trivial (but easy to identify) against the critical (but needing more work to understand) is, I think, a fundamental problem in delivering effective workplace health and safety management organisations. In my view, and consistent with my comments about intent earlier, I think organisations need to take very deliberate steps to articulate what is critical or crucial in workplace health and safety management and ensure that the majority of workplace health and safety management activity is directed to understanding and assuring those critical or crucial processes.

ONE OFF DEPARTURES

Another important aspect to my mind when it comes to assuring workplace health and safety management, is to continually question whether issues that we see in workplace health and safety management are one-off departures from an otherwise effective system, or whether they are, or are indicative of, potential systemic failure.

It is one thing to identify that a worker did not comply with the safety procedure, but it is another thing altogether to identify that half of the workforce did not know about the correct method to perform a task as was the case in Fry v Keating.

Similar to my comments about incident investigations earlier, I think one of the most straightforward things an organisation can do to obtain a better understanding of the efficacy of their workplace health and safety management systems is to include questions and observations about one-off departures v systemic failures in incident investigations and health and safety reports.

It would seem to me to make perfect sense to include a term of reference in every incident investigation asking whether the incident was a one-off departure from the organisation's expectations, or whether there is any evidence that the incident, or elements of it, might represent a systemic failure.

Similarly, health and safety reports that identify problems or concerns in relation to workplace health and safety management should also identify whether those problems or concerns represent a one-off departure or could be indicative of systemic failure.

TESTING, VERIFYING, ASSUMPTION AND CORRUPTION

I have made the point several times in this book that systems to manage workplace health and safety are subject to assumption and organisational corruption. I believe that is true.

I also believe that my proposed framework for proving safety is just as susceptible to assumption and organisational corruption as any other workplace health and safety management process.

However, I also believe that a narrative framework for reporting workplace health and safety can be verified and tested to understand and expose assumptions and organisational corruption in a way that traditional workplace health and safety reporting and metrics cannot.

For example, if there is an incident in an organisation that highlights a workers lack of risk awareness or hazard awareness associated with their task, it is very difficult to go back and unpick a metric like the number of Take 5s completed, or the percentage of JHA's completed, or the number of management conversation conducted – all of which could theoretically have information about worker knowledge of hazards associated with their tasks. We would need to unpick those metrics to try and identify whether our systems to ensure workers had good *"hazard or risk literacy"* were fit for purpose, implemented and effective. We would need to unpick the metrics because typically, none of the metrics have examples, indicators, or any explanation of the level of confidence in the indicator or the activities that sit behind them.

In contrast, under the framework I have described, something like the workforce's hazard and risk literacy should be identified as a crucial system, and subject to ongoing examination through health and safety reporting, with the occasional deep dive analysis. A narrative inquiry which explains the process an organisation went through to test and examine the quality of hazard and risk understanding associated with tasks across the organisation, coupled with the express findings of incident investigation directed to the specific question of proper systems and adequate supervision, can be revisited and analysed. It is also a process that can be replicated by the organisation or external parties as a verification exercise and to get confidence about the process. Further, the specific incident itself can be tested against the findings from the previous narrative inquiry or reports to test and confirm whether the incident aligns with any observations from the earlier finding, or whether the incident represents a significant departure from the findings. If the incident represents a significant departure from the findings that should lead to proactive measures on the part of the organisation to further deep dives the issue and validate the organisation's understanding of it.

In short, if the organisation produces narrative reports that examine critical or crucial workplace health and safety management systems, those reports can be examined, questioned, tested, and verified. A third party can be brought into the organisation to conduct a similar (or identical) review to confirm whether the organisation's narrative reports are a valid representation about what is happening in the organisation.

A green traffic light in a monthly health and safety report that indicates the correct number of Take 5s were done during a reporting period cannot be verified in the same way.

FINAL THOUGHTS

I think the evidence is compelling that our current approach to measuring and assuring workplace health and safety systems is not fit for purpose. Certainly, from the narrow perspective of legal risk management, workplace health and safety metrics and reporting do not provide any insight into the organisation's level of legal compliance, and none of the information produced by organisations to measure and assure workplace health and safety management systems are any use in defending legal proceedings.

A framework for proving safety

If our processes of health and safety reporting and measurement cannot meet the (apparent) minimum expectation of legal compliance, can they really tell us anything about the state of health and safety in workplaces? I suspect not.

My proposal for an alternative framework of proving safety is designed to move organisations away from unhelpful metric collation and shift workplace health and safety assurance into a permanent research project.

The fundamentals of proving safety in this context include:

- a clear intent to understand if our systems for managing workplace health and safety are fit for of purpose, implemented and effective;
- capacity building to drive safety literacy in the organisation;
- a focus on criticality;
- a drive to improve the quality of workplace health and safety management assurance by doing less workplace health and safety activities, but doing them better;
- a recognition of understanding the importance of distinguishing between one-off departures from our workplace health and safety management systems and those matters which could be indicators of potential systemic failure; and
- a willingness to recognise and surface the impact of assumptions and organisational corruption on our workplace health and safety management systems.

I recognise what I am proposing is a fundamental, if not radical, shift in thinking about workplace health and safety management and assurance. I am not especially confident about the willingness of organisations to move as far as I am suggesting.

However, if I could suggest two less challenging but to my mind immeasurably useful shifts in thinking it would be, first, add the following specific terms of reference to your incident investigations:

- Did the processes designed to prevent or manage the incident comply with any regulations, codes of practice or guidance material produced by the regulator that were relevant to the incident?
- Before the incident, what evidence did the organisation have that the processes designed to prevent or manage the incident actually complied with any regulations, codes of practice or guidance material produced by the regulator that were relevant to the incident?

- Prior to the incident what evidence did the organisation have that the processes designed to prevent or manage the incident were implemented and effective to manage this type of incident?

Second, whenever a health and safety report raises an issue or concern about workplace health and safety management it should specifically address the following two questions:

- whether the workplace health and safety management systems that apply to the issue or concern were consistent with regulations, codes of practice or guidance material provided by the regulator; and
- what evidence is there that the workplace health and safety management systems that apply to the issue or concern are implemented and effective to manage the issue or concern?

In the end, it seems to me to be a fundamental obligation of organisations, their leaders, and the people who provide the technical workplace health and safety expertise in an organisation to have, first and foremost in their mind, a willingness and desire to interrogate and challenge themselves and their organisation to effectively and conclusively ...

Prove the Effectiveness of their Crucial Systems

A framework for proving safety

Annexure 1
Legal Professional Privilege

Legal professional privilege

A fundamental tenet of good workplace health and safety management is communication between the organisation and workers, and a critical aspect of this communication is sharing lessons from incidents. Legal professional privilege effectively stops an organisation sharing information about an incident with their workforce if they want to maintain the privilege.

Legal professional privilege protects confidential communications between a lawyer and their client. Ordinarily *"communications"* such as letters, emails, reports, diary notes, file notes, hazard reports, incident investigations or even conversations are *"discoverable"* in legal proceedings. This means they must be handed over/disclosed to regulators or other third parties as part of legal proceedings.

Communications that are subject to legal professional privilege do not have to be handed over.

The theory behind legal professional privilege is to ensure clients can get proper legal advice. In this way it helps in the administration of justice.

If conversations between lawyers and their clients had to be handed over to 3rd parties, then clients would be very reluctant to tell their lawyer the truth, and lawyers could not give their clients full and frank advice.

Legal professional privilege covers confidential communications that are made for the dominant purpose of receiving legal advice, or in reasonable anticipation of legal proceedings.

Legal professional privilege does not cover communications which are not made for the *"dominant purpose"*. In the context of a workplace accident, documents that are created before the accident will not be covered by Privilege. This typically includes:

- training records;
- policies and procedures;
- hazard reports;
- emails and other internal communications;
- audits;
- job hazard analysis or similar risk assessment documents;
- safe work method statements; or
- earlier incident investigations.

If a communication has been brought into existence for more than one reason, then obtaining legal advice is probably not the dominant purpose. For example, after an accident you may create an incident investigation, but this could be for a multitude of purposes, including:

- complying with your own safe work procedures or other health and safety processes;
- complying with your own incident investigation procedures;
- complying with contractual requirements with a client, or updating a client about incident;
- notifying a regulator; or
- providing advice to senior management or board.

Legal professional privilege in the context of health and safety is complicated and can be. difficult to maintain mostly because workplace health and safety related communications are usually created for a multitude of reasons, not for seeking legal advice.

Seeking legal advice is a fundamental element of establishing legal professional privilege, so the organisation must engage with a lawyer, and you must engage early. A health and safety manager cannot create legal professional privilege by themselves, and communications are not covered by legal professional privilege just because you want your lawyer to look at them.

Importantly, even if an organisation establishes legal professional privilege over communications, the privilege can be lost.

A common way that legal professional privilege is lost (or waived) is when the communication loses its confidentiality. For example, if confidential communications are shared with the workforce, a client or other third parties it may no longer be confidential and no longer covered by legal professional privilege.

In the wake of a serious workplace accident there is often a great deal of tension in an organisation between sharing information (which is consistent with good safety management) and keeping information confidential (which is consistent with good legal risk management). This will never be an easy path to navigate.

Legal professional privilege only protects your organisation's communications. It does not protect an organisation from legal proceedings or investigation. Workplace health and safety regulators have wide ranging powers to investigate workplace accidents, and the exercise of those powers cannot be stopped by legal professional privilege. All legal professional privilege does is stop a regulator accessing communications which are covered by the privilege.

Often, in the aftermath of a serious workplace accident people will generate all manner of communications – emails, file notes, telephone calls, preliminary witness statements – before they stop and think about the best way to manage the incident. Organisations recognise that people are not familiar with serious workplace accidents and may not know the best way to respond, and for this reason they develop emergency response plans to help guide the process. In the same way, people are not familiar with the legal consequences of serious workplace accidents, and it is a good idea to set up criteria and processes for considering and establishing legal professional privilege before a serious workplace accident so that people know how to respond.

By way of summary:

- legal professional privilege protects confidential communications between a lawyer and their client;
- legal professional privilege applies to confidential communications brought into existence for the dominant purpose of getting legal advice or in anticipation of legal proceedings;
- communications that have been created for multiple reasons, or before legal professional privilege was established, will not be covered by the privilege; and
- legal professional privilege can be waived or lost.

Notwithstanding the tensions that legal professional privilege can create in an organisation between sharing and withholding information, ultimately legal professional privilege is a decision for an organisation: it is not mandatory and establishing or not establishing legal professional privilege is not the same thing as complying with an organisation's obligations under work health and safety legislation.